The Teen Years - Don't Get Mad - Get Through It

-A parent's guide to surviving the teenage years without tearing your hair out.....

By

Sarah Newton

Cover art by Jemma Pentney

Editing by Terry Stark

Chapters

Reviews

"Sarah's book has brought a little more peace and calm to our house, it's like having a teenager's perspective wrapped up in an adult brain! Thank you Sarah" *Sharon Campone-Evans*

"This book is written for parents struggling to understand their teenager and therefore struggling in their relationship with them. The content is written from the point of view that the teenager is NOT their behaviour and that as such, their behaviour is not to be taken personally by the parent. It gives explanation about the brain development of a teenager in a way that is easily understood, giving the reasoning behind the teenager's behaviour which supports the parent's understanding; giving way to compassion for self (as a parent) and teenager in what can be a very challenging time.

The book gives practical steps that can be put in place to deal with situations that may arise between parents and teens which, when used, deals with the situation in an effective way whilst maintaining and supporting a positive relationship. The book also presents some in-depth questions for the parent to explore their own self awareness, should they wish to do so.

Written in a simple, easy to read format, using every day language the author uses their own real life examples to convey how to put the practical steps in place for upmost effectiveness.

Overall, this book offers valuable advice and guidance for parents, which when followed step by step supports parents influencing their teenager in a way that is empowering to both parties in the parents/teenager relationship." *Tracy Parker*

Dedication

This book is dedicated to my wonderful teenager whom I love and adore and my little teenage in training. Bronte and Freya you teach me so much about life and myself and without you this book would not be here. Eddie my eternal teenager, I love and adore you so much, you are my rock.

Acknowledgements

I would like to acknowledge a few people who supported me to complete this book. Firstly, my clients who have constantly asked me for a resource like the one I have created here. To my sister (and brother)-in-law who helped my words make sense and gave me some great advice. To my designer Jemma who created a wonderful visual for this book. And finally, to everyone who has stood by and supported me throughout my long and exciting journey.

Introduction

The teenage years can feel like a never-ending cycle of disagreements, arguing and endless repetition. I know; I am going through them with my daughter at the moment. You can end up feeling frustrated, exhausted and alone. Your earlier dreams of raising a happy, healthy, confident child turn into, "Please let me just get through this day without another row!" If only they would listen to you, do as you ask. I mean, how on earth are they going to take responsibility and cope on their own? You can feel like you are turning into a nag. That is why I wrote this book. Parents all over the world were telling me they needed quick, easy-to-use information that they could implement straight away. The needed practical advice and they needed it now. This content-rich book will lead you through the most common problems I get asked in this field and give you easy-to-use strategies. I will even walk you through what to do if it goes wrong.

Why is parenting teens so hard?

There are many reasons. Partly due to the change in the teen's brain structure and their natural instinct to buck against the family system, but without a shadow of a doubt, in my experience the transition to the teen years is so difficult because most parents have not moved forward with their teenager and are stuck in their managing role that they took on so well before. When things start going wrong in the teen years, parents do more of what they did before; to try and get their teenager to behave better.

THE PROBLEM IS THAT WHAT YOU DID BEFORE WILL NOT WORK NOW. YOU NEED A WHOLE NEW APPROACH.

And that is what we concentrate on in this book; the necessary changes in your thought process and approach to get the very best out of the techniques I will teach you. In my 18 years in this field, I have learnt that for every technique you implement, if your thinking and emotions are not in line with that technique it will fail so. We do a lot of work in this book; working on the Inner Parent, so when you implement these strategies they will work.

This book is designed to be used over 10 weeks; each week you read one chapter, implement what it says then move on to the next chapter the next week. However, it is up to you to decide the speed you use, so work at a pace that feels right for you and fits in with your life. You can dip in and out as you wish; however, it is essential that you implement the actions suggested or you will not get the full benefit of this experience. I expect you to work hard and do what is required; results will not come for free. I will be with you every step of the way, but for this to be effective you must put in the work. I require all the parents I work with to fully commit to changing their situation; this is yours and your child's future life and happiness together and I take that very seriously. I am 100% committed to you and your success.

Each chapter is simple and easy to follow and includes:

- Your 3-minute daily emotional workout

- Your 2-minute brain workout

- Your 1-minute implementation exercise

All chapters also include sections:

- Help! Why is my teenager acting this way – background information and knowledge into why this may be happening and what you can do to ease the strain.

- Help! It has all gone wrong – what to do if things don't quite go the way you planned.

- Extra Credit – for those parents who are ultra brave and want to take it even further.

If you're ready to stop the never-ending cycle of disagreements, arguing and repeating yourself endlessly, then I am ready to support you.

Let's get going

The transition to the Teen Years - Why are the teen years so difficult?

The transition to the teen years can be a painful and difficult one. As parents, you need to help them navigate these waters. But how do you help them do that? First, you need to understand a little about what is happening during these years.

During my years of experience working with young people, the significance of school Year 9 (13/14 years old) has become increasingly apparent. The difference between a Year 7 or 8 and a Year 9 is immense and I believe that Year 9 is the critical one; what happens here may influence the rest of the child's schooling. So why is it significant?

I believe there are many reasons; let me share one with you:

TRANSITIONS.

The teen years contain some of the most important life transition stages, i.e. school to college and school to work. These transitions cause stress for the teens as they search for a new sense of balance in their lives. Let me explain how this works. Any transition has three stages and, each one, from start to finish, can take three years. These stages are System, Stress and Balance. I'd like us to look at these one by one.

System

We live, whether we like it or not, within a series of systems – family systems, work systems, society systems and, of course, for teenagers, a school system. Each system has its own goals and interests, which may not necessarily be the same as the individual's goals and interests. For example, the school has a system of wearing a school uniform, which may not be a system with which the child agrees; the family has certain systems which, as the teenager grows and develops, may not match their own. As a child gains abstract thought (at approximately 13 years: Year 9) they begin to question these systems and the goals and interests within. This is not rebellion, just testing; they need to question each system to see if it is one they want to carry forward into adulthood or not. The teenager begins to separate their system self from their true selves and, of course, some conflict follows.

For a parent this means that suddenly things the teenager used to do and like, change. Parenting styles that use to work no longer have any effect. These changes are why teens are increasingly more interested in their friends (who are also in this conflict). This can make parents panic and try even more to enforce a system, which in turn causes more conflict. As a parent at this stage you need to take more of a consultative approach with your teenager, looking at what they would want to change and coming to agreeable outcomes. This will be far more beneficial for all concerned and will in fact teach the teenager that they do indeed have control over their lives and the decisions they make.

Stress

The teenager's separation of the system-self to their true self causes them a huge amount of stress. The teenager begins to realise the increasing disparity between their system-self and their true self and does not know what to do about it. They begin to focus only in the short term, are driven by status symbols, have outer-directed priorities and have reactive decision making, which to an adult in the balance stage is hard to comprehend. In this stage, the teen is in a relentless rush, never stopping to catch breath. As a parent, just recognizing this stage can take the pressure off you both. Knowing that what they are doing is just a natural progression and not a fault in our parenting is help enough! Supporting them to make decisions on what is important to them and supporting them to get a greater sense of self is very helpful in this stage.

Balance

As the young person matures and begins to make sense of their system-self and true self and integrate the two, they reach balance; they know who they are and what they are good at. They are more focused on the long-term; they have meaning and are inner-directed. Clarification that they will eventually achieve the desired balance is helpful.

For instance, a very disruptive Year 9 student can, in Year 11, become resigned to the fact that they don't behave in English because they are "not very good at it", as one student said to me today – whether right or wrong, that is what he had identified to be his true self. This is why when a child is 13 or 14 we need to be very careful what we say to them about their capabilities. If we tell them at this crucial stage that they are not good at certain things then they may choose that as one of their "systems" and carry it forward to adult life.

Information based on Don't Waste Your Talent – Bob McDonald and Don Hutcheson.

Understanding the teenage years

Before we start, I want to give you a little background so you can understand and begin to appreciate the situation you and your teenager are in. Most parents tell me that the emergence of the teenage alien is almost instant. One day they put their beloved to bed as a child, the next morning, the child who wakes up is a teenage alien. Why? To understand this change, let's take a brief look at your different roles in your child's development:

0 to 6 years: Teacher Role

Think of the first six years of your parenting life as you being a teacher to your child, teaching them everything they need to know, to gain all the information for later life. This is the stage where your precious baby needs to learn everything from you, the adult in their lives. This is often the stage most enjoyed by parents.

7 to 12 years: Manager Role

The next stage starts between ages six and seven when a child moves from 'learning to read' to 'reading to learn' and as your child moves through this phase, you become a manager in their lives, the administrator, so to speak, as they begin to initiate activities and become more social. Your child's social circle moves beyond just you and they turn to other sources to learn about life. These years are far less demanding of the parent and it is during this time that the parent is setting the stage for the teenage years to come. Learning to handle the discussions about small tasks like washing up at this stage is essential before you try to deal with the drugs and sex conversations in the years to come.

13 years onwards: Coaching Role

When your children approach thirteen, something even more extraordinary happens and their cognitive ability begins to develop. They begin to realise that life exists outside their own world, and begin to experience emotions that they have never experienced before. They become unsure about themselves and their new level of thinking. The teenage alien begins to emerge as they try harder and harder to make sense of their new 'humanness'. They shut off from the outside world, choosing alien-type behaviour as a defence mechanism until they themselves find out what it is to be human. During this stage, the parent needs to move with the teenager into a different communication style. Your teenager no longer requires you in your former role; you are now needed in a more supportive role. Try to manage and control your child and you will get nowhere. As a parent you need to manage yourself first, so you in turn can be the support to your teenager. Your teenager no longer wants you to manage them; they need you to coach them. As you have bought this book, my guess is that you are stuck in your old manager role, but the manager has been fired and you are no longer sure what your job is. As you try to manage more, your teenager moves further away from you. Let go of the manager — it's time to move on. My job is to encourage you to grow with your teenager and for you to adopt more of a coaching role.

Have fun, your journey is just beginning.

Understanding the Teenage Brain

I think to parent in the best possible way it is very useful for us to understand what is happening inside the brains of our 'little darlings'. While it does not excuse bad behaviour, at least it makes sense of it for us a little and helps us appreciate the situation more.

The parts of the brain most affected in the teenage years are:

- Cerebral cortex - logical and spatial reasoning, i.e., thinking through the consequences of actions.

- Temporal cortex – responsible for language.

- Frontal Lobe (internal policeman) - future planning, resisting impulses and balancing the social, emotional and intellectual parts of the self.

However, the most important factor is the move from concrete to abstract thought process. In young people, this kind of thought process does not begin to develop until about 12 in girls and 14 in boys. Until a child has abstract thinking, they cannot successfully answer complex questions or use rationale effectively.

Abstract thinking is a level of thinking about things that is removed from the facts of here and now and from specific concrete examples of things or concepts. Abstract thinkers are able to reflect on events and ideas, on attributes and relationships separate from the objects that have those attributes or share those relationships. Thus, for example, a concrete thinker can think about this particular dog; a more abstract thinker can think about dogs in general. A concrete thinker can think about this dog on this rug; a more abstract thinker can think about spatial relations, like "on". A concrete thinker can see that this ball is big; a more abstract thinker can think about size in general. A concrete thinker can count three biscuits; a more abstract thinker can think about numbers. A concrete thinker can recognize that John likes Betty; a more abstract thinker can reflect on emotions, like affection. This is the reason why, if we ask a child with concrete thought what they want to do when they grow up, they are likely to state something they know, a job their parent does or a teacher, and as a child grows into abstract thought this is likely to change significantly.

This development of abstract thought really impacts on how we parent and the questions we will ask the person in front of us. The logical questions that appear natural to us are likely to get an insufficient response from a child without abstract thought and they are much more likely to just answer what they think we want to hear versus what they really want to say, simply because they don't understand the question. When asking questions to a child without abstract thought we need to be certain in what we ask, giving choices and leading the question slightly.

In my first session with a youth client I am always trying to establish how developed their thought process is by asking them a mixture of abstract and concrete questions.

Concrete: What subjects do you like at school?

Abstract: How do you see your school subject's helping you in the future?

If I come away feeling as if I have had an adult conversation with the client, then their thought process is fully developed. If not, I just know that I need to guide more than coach.

This thought process has a huge impact on our parenting and we need to adjust accordingly.

Week One

How to say 'No' confidently and deal with any repercussions.

Welcome to the first week of your programme. This week we will be working together to help you say 'No' more confidently and also feel empowered and able to deal with any repercussions that may come from that.

This chapter contains:

1. Your 3-minute daily emotional workout

2. Your 2-minute brain workout

3. Your 1-minute implementation exercise

4. Help! Why is my teenager acting this way? Background information and knowledge into why this may be happening and what you can do to ease the strain.

5. Help! It has all gone wrong! What to do if things don't quite go the way you planned.

6. Extra Credit – for those parents who are ultra brave and want to take it even further.

As always, it is up to you how you work through the chapter. There is no hard and fast rule; each person will work at their own pace and in their own manner. Take what resonates most for you from this lesson and start there. The questions in each chapter are designed to allow you to self-coach and will deepen the learning and experience for you.

The Myth of 'No'

I feel blessed as a parent to have coaching skills and be able to use them in my own home, and I think they help so much in this area. Before coaching, I was a 'Noaholic' and I loved the word 'No', using it at every opportunity to exert myself. I had grown up feeling like I needed to force my opinion on others and stand up for what I believed as right, so saying 'No' and showing my displeasure was something I did really well. It was only when my daughter Bronte was three that I began to question my use of 'No'. There was one particular day when I found myself in the garden out in the sun, just relaxing and having fun with her when I caught myself just saying 'No' constantly. "Bronte, no, don't do that, don't do this..." I began to get bored of hearing it myself. So I decided the next day to count up the times I said 'No' to her in one day. This was simple, by the way; I just got a counter and every time I found myself saying 'No', I clicked. Just over 200 times; 200 a day is enough to severely impact on a life, by anyone's standards!

Experts suggest that children need to hear approximately four positive statements for every negative comment to counterbalance the impact of negative comments, and you can guarantee I wasn't saying yes to her 800 times! I was shocked, to say the least, and decided that from that day forward I would have a 'Yes' attitude, and I would always say yes to her (more later). I have to say it changed my relationship with her, lowered my stress levels and changed my parenting for good.

What is a 'No'?

Put simply, 'No' is the act of refusing someone's request, it's that simple. So every time a request is made of us we have the right to say Yes, No or Maybe, whatever our age.

I think we choose to say 'No' far too easily and often we say 'No' when we really mean something else or we are just trying to stop the conversation.

We are taught that 'no means no', but in my experience working with my clients, 'No' often means a variety of things such as:

- I am too busy to deal with this; ask me another time

- I don't want to think about this at the moment

- I don't know what to do so I want this to go away

- I feel so hurt by you in the past that I want to punish you

- Feel so unequipped to deal with this situation and unable to deal with the consequences.

Have you ever noticed the different ways people say 'No', the energy they put into the word or don't put into the word? Saying 'No' to a child who is about to touch the fire has a very different energy from saying 'No' to a child who is asking for a sweet. In my opinion, the 'No' that we say to the fire, the definite 'No', should be the only one we are using. And of course, sometimes 'No' just means plain old 'No'. We have heard the request, thought about it and we want to say 'No'.

Saying 'No' is a very confrontational way to behave with our children, particularly our teenagers and is bound to always end up in an argument. I don't know about you, but arguing is not my favourite thing and if I have to do it I really want to save it for something worthwhile and worthy of my attention.

Having a 'Yes' attitude!

Since deciding to always say 'yes', I have found parenting has become so much easier and certainly my clients say the same too. Saying 'yes' is not about giving in and looking weak, it is about being open and honest and asking yourself what would need to happen for you to say 'yes' in a particular situation. When we ask that question we get a very different answer. I remember when Bronte was 12 years-old and she came home one day all excited, asking me if she could go to a 16th birthday party with her friend that finished at 11pm.My initial reaction was that Bronte was too young; I don't even know the girl whose party it is. The only time I spoke to her, I thought she sounded 'rough', which provoked many reactions in my head. Fear, mostly. Bronte does not know how to cope in the real world, what if someone gives her drink, drugs, etc? What am I going to do? Say no, she is too young; Eddie, my husband, won't like this, and what about the effect on Freya, her younger sister? My frantic thought process (yes, I am human) was broken by, "Mum, please can I?" OK, panic again now, what do I do? She wants an answer. Luckily, this is where the coach in me kicks in!

OK, get real, you need more time to think before you answer… stall.

"Bronte, I need a bit of time to think about this, let's talk about it later".

Phew, I had fended her off for a while, so now I could think about what I wanted to say. So, what was really going on? Well, I was frightened that she could not cope with situations that came up so I needed reassurance…I needed to speak with her later.

"Bronte, I want you to be happy, it is just that I am concerned that you are too young. This is the first teenage party you have been to and I am not sure you could handle certain situations that might arise".

She then went through a list of such situations and told me how she would deal with each and every one of them. Now that had me snookered, yet I still did not feel right, so I told her I would make a decision by Thursday.

Thursday morning and I still was not sure, so I told her I would tell her later and as I sat at my computer it became clear. I asked myself one question.

If it was xxxxx (the sensible friend, not the friend with the 'rough accent) asking her to go, what would I say?

I realised that I would have answered yes, so my problem was not with Bronte, it was the judgment I was making about the friend which, let's face it, was not fair at all.

Response

So I sent her a simple text. You may go to the ball Cinderella......

So what can you learn from that? How would you have responded?

And it can work in all kinds of situations from the smallest to the biggest.

"Mum, can I have a packet of crisps?"

What needs to happen so that I can say 'yes'? Well I am worried about their health, crisps are not particularly nutritious and they haven't had their fruit and veg today...

So we could answer,

"Yes, but I need you to eat an apple first" or "Yes, after dinner"

"Mum, can I have a friend stay over? "

What needs to happen so that I can say 'yes'? well the house is a mess and I have nothing in for dinner and I don't want to be disturbed as there is something on that I want to watch.

"Yes, however first you need to quickly clean the house for me, nip to the shops to get some extra food and I will ask the pair of you to amuse yourselves in your bedroom for the evening because there's something I really want to watch on TV."

It is not that we should never say 'No', just that there needs to be a reason for it! And if you don't have the time to think about it or make a decision there and then it is OK to say, "I need more time to think about this, if you continue to ask me then I will have to say no. I will have a decision for you by XXXX"

I think having a 'Yes' attitude allows us to get clear what is important to us as a parent and empowers us to make decisions that are great for our family. It also stops a lot of the negotiating, which young people do so well. When your child knows that you have thought about it and that a No means No, then things become much easier. Often, we are so unclear as parents and change our mind so much that children know that a No simply means maybe, so they keep going, they negotiate around everything and drive you mad until you say yes. This can make us feel disempowered and like a failure, all because we were not clear in the first place.

It means that when we say No, we say No with confidence and power and because of this it is more likely to be accepted.

The other morning I was walking somewhere with my daughter, who had, initially protested about going. I said to her, "You know, when I said you couldn't stay at home this morning by yourself and you had to come with me, you didn't complain; thanks for that!" She replied, "It's OK Mum, because I know that when you say No that you really mean it, and there's a good reason for it."

And this is what this is all about, saying 'No' and meaning it. A 'No' that can't be negotiated and doesn't really mean anything else. For me, navigating the teen years is all about not putting fuel on their fire. Most teens are constantly harbouring embers, waiting to be ignited, so when we add fuel by saying No, we get a flare up. When we say yes, we add water to these embers, meaning that your child has nothing to ignite, nothing to spark from, which all sounds good to me.

Your 3-minute emotional workout

For me, working on your emotional stuff is the key to being a strong and powerful parent. However, it is not easy. When you are doing these emotional exercises, don't get too involved with what comes up. Just notice that it is interesting and let it go. We have a tendency to navel gaze, feel sorry and think there is something wrong with us. We all have stuff - emotional baggage - and to move forward all we have to do is notice it and move on.

Firstly, I want you to find a quiet space where you will not be disturbed and take three deep breaths; this will just balance you.

Then I just want you to sit with these three questions. Just ask them of yourself and notice what comes up in terms of thoughts, feelings and emotions.

1. What does the word No mean to me?

2. Why do I want to say No?

3. What scares me about saying Yes?

If you get nothing coming up then that is fine too, just come back to it another day.

Just sit for three minutes and after that, have a notebook to hand and just quickly jot down the thoughts, feelings or emotions that comes up for you.

Your two minute thinking exercise.

I say 'thinking', but I am going to be asking you to write too.

Getting all the feelings out to do with a situation will really support you in moving forward.

Get a pen and paper and the pad you used to jot down your observations from the above exercise.

Then just answer these questions on the paper; write as much or as little as you feel.

1. What was the one thought, feeling or emotion stuck in my mind from the previous exercise?

2. What makes this so poignant for me?

3. How is it impacting my relationship with my child now?

Then just sit, take a few breaths and release.

Your implementation exercise.

I want you to do one thing today and that is simply to challenge yourself to say yes all day to the things that are definite. Find your own language around them and say yes. When you can complete this exercise, come back to these questions.

1. How did it feel saying yes this week?

2. What was great about it?

3. What was not so great about it?

Help! Why is my teenager acting this way?

Mostly, teenagers don't respond well to no because, let's face it, no one likes a no. However, for teenagers it is mostly due to parents not being clear. They know that a no never really means no, so they are always pushing their luck. Also, as we mentioned in "The transition to the Teen Years" a teenager's job is to test the system and see the limits of it. For them to fully integrate themselves as adults, they have to buck up against their family system to see which values, principles and beliefs they want to take forward with them. So partly, it is their job to disagree. Also, if you look at brain development there are two factors that make our children less cooperative. Firstly, when they develop abstract thought process they begin to question everything around them, they begin to realise they have a voice and a life outside their closed family and friends, they begin to question their place in the world and in turn this makes them less cooperative. Also, their frontal lobe is changing and as we learnt in brain development, the frontal lobe is the internal policeman, the one that tells us to slow down, so where they could previously have seen that going on and on would annoy their parents, maybe now it is not so obvious to them. Also, dopamine levels in the brain are dropping, so their need for excitement increases and, indeed, nothing fires them up more than a good argument.

Help! It has all gone wrong!

OK, firstly don't panic, it is nothing that can't be undone. If everything does go wrong it is probably just due to a lack of clarity and consistency. So ask yourself, was I clear in my statements? If not, you need to rectify it and this can be by just saying, "You know what, I wasn't clear, what I meant to say was XXXX." We must never be frightened of admitting that we made a mistake. The same with consistency; if you feel you have been consistent in this matter then fine, if not then go back and apologise. Then ask yourself if your No was a fair No and be really honest with yourself. If not, go back and say, "You know, I said No without really thinking about this. I would love to say Yes but certain conditions have to exist to enable me to do so." And if it is just that they don't like the No, you just need to hang in there, this will get a bit worse before it gets better. It is just like working out; the first time we do it is hard and we ache afterwards, but the more we do it, the easier it will get.

If you have said No and your child has blown their top, then this is most likely because before it has got them the results they wanted, so they pull out all the stops this time. You have to stay factual and not get tied up in all the emotions. You need to say, "I have said No, I am not going to change my mind, no matter what you do." Say that a few times and if the behaviours continues, say, "Stop that, you are angry because I said No and no matter how much you do that, I am not going to change my mind. If you continue to do this then..." Then you must tell them what will happen; this will be something you can do and you are in charge of, not something you will do to them. For example, you may walk away, leave the house, call their Dad and possibly, in extreme cases, call the police if the behaviour is violent. However hard it is, you must stay focused, factual and consistent. Only by doing this will it get better. Yes, you can give in to make things easier, but all you will be doing is making things more difficult for yourself in the future. The choice is yours; if you want this to change you have to put the hard work in now.

Extra Credit!

How we parent is how we were parented and often, by just examining the patterns that we have taken on, we can move forward greatly in our own personal lives.

So I want you to take yourself to a spot where you feel safe and secure and can be alone and undisturbed and just ask yourself these questions. You can just be with them in thought or write down your answers.

- Did my parents or anyone else say 'No' a lot to me as a child?

- How did it make me feel?

- Did I feel I was listened to as a child?

- Are any of these experiences impacting how I parent?

- Are any of these experiences impacting how I parent?

- Am I trying to put something right from my past through how I parent? If so, is this realistic and helpful for me?

As before, just let what comes to the surface come up; don't judge it or make yourself wrong.

Then ask yourself if you are willing to let go of this feeling.

If so, take a few deep breaths and feel where it is in your body and imagine that you are being cleaned like a valet would clean a car. Imagine them cleaning that piece out of you, or imagine it floating away like a balloon.

Week Two

How to build respect in your home.

Welcome to your second week in this programme. This week we will be working together to build up respect in your home.

This chapter contains:

This chapter contains:

1.   Your 3-minute daily emotional workout

2.   Your 2-minute brain workout

3.   Your 1-minute implementation exercise

4.   Help! Why is my teenager acting this way? Background information and knowledge into why this may be happening and what you can do to ease the strain.

5.   Help! It has all gone wrong! What to do if things don't quite go the way you planned.

6.   Extra Credit – for those parents who are ultra brave and want to take it even further.

As always it is up to you how you work through the chapter; there is no hard and fast rule, each person will work at their own pace and in their own manner. Take what resonates most for you from this lesson and start there.

The questions in each chapter are designed to allow you to self-coach and will deepen the learning and experience for you.

How to build up respect in your home

No Respect

When parents tell me that there is no respect in their home, what they are really telling me is that their child is not doing what they want; they are calling this a lack of respect. It seems to me that we have gone far beyond those Good Old Days of children respecting their elders just because they are old; or maybe that is just me! There is a difference between being respectful and showing respect; one is demanded and the other earned. If we want to build respect in our home then I think we have to look at everything we do and ask, is it respectful? We have to become respectful to breed respect and we have to believe we deserve respect and are worthy of it before we can even begin to build it. As a child I was often called disrespectful, which was most annoying as I really didn't see myself as that. I had manners, I was nice; it is just that I had an opinion and I stuck up for myself. Just because an adult told me to jump I didn't ask how high, I asked why? However, my mum begged to differ and was always telling me that I didn't respect her. What I now realise is that she was saying that I made her feel bad. She was making it my fault for the way she felt. She was, in essence, blaming me for her misery; how can that be right? She was giving me her power and doing a great job of playing the victim and, you guessed it, the more I knew it annoyed her, the more I did it. And so the never ending cycle began. Most children labelled as disrespectful are merely opinionated, strong willed and not afraid to speak up, which is a great quality and may often be what is missing in the parent or what the parent wished they could have or be like. It isn't really fair to blame our children for a perceived fault in ourselves.

So when parents say that their children have no respect, often they are saying:

- My child will not do what I say

- My child is too outspoken and it is embarrassing

- My child is not behaving in the way I think they should be

- My child is pushing my buttons and I don't know what to do.

- My child is pushing my buttons and I don't know what to do.

If you look at the word respect it means to hold someone in high esteem. Isn't that not a great way for us to hold family members? It does not say it is something that is deserved. When we hold someone in high esteem, does that mean we will always agree and do what they say? No, that would be blindly following; it means we treat them in a respectful way, which means we don't swear, shout, or a host of other things. We need to get really clear on what respect means to us as a family and what a respectful house would look like.

Your 3-minute emotional workout

For me, working on your emotional stuff is the key to being a strong and powerful parent. However, it is not easy. When you are doing these emotional exercises, don't get too involved with what comes up. Just notice that it is interesting and let it go. We have a tendency to navel gaze, feel sorry and think there is something wrong with us. We all have stuff - emotional baggage - and to move forward all we have to do is notice it and move on.

Firstly, I want you to find a quiet space where you will not be disturbed and take three deep breaths; this will just balance you.

Then I just want you to sit with these questions. Just ask them of yourself and notice what comes up in terms of thoughts, feelings and emotions.

1. What does respect mean to me?

2. How do I feel when I hear the word?

3. What was the message I got about respect as a child?

4. How do I show myself that I respect myself?

If you get nothing come up then that is fine too; just come back to it another day.

Just sit for three minutes and after that, have a notebook to hand and quickly jot down the thoughts, feelings or emotions that comes up for you.

Your two minute thinking exercise.

I say 'thinking', but I am going to be asking you to write too.

Getting all the feelings out to do with a situation will really support you in moving forward.

Get a pen and paper and the pad you used to jot down your observations from the above exercise.

Then just answer these questions on the paper; write as much or as little as you feel.

1. What was the one thought, feeling or emotion stuck in my mind from the previous exercise?

2. What makes this so poignant for me?

3. How is it impacting my relationship with my child now?

Then just sit, take a few breaths and release.

Your implementation exercise.

I want you to make a list of the top five things that your child does that you feel are disrespectful, in terms of your definition of respect. Then when they do this thing next time, here is what I want you to do.

As an example, let us imagine that your child has just sworn at you.

Step 1 – "Do you realise you are swearing at me? Please stop.

Most will stop after this first stage.

Step Two – "I have asked you to stop swearing at me. It is really disrespectful; I don't swear at you and I don't expect you to swear at me. Please stop. Incidentally, best if you're telling the truth here - don't swear at them!

Help! Why is my teenager acting this way?

Most teenagers don't set out to be disrespectful; it is not their aim in life or their preferred method of interacting, whatever you may think. In my experience, when teenagers act disrespectfully it is either down to a culture in the home of disrespect, or because they are dealing with some issue and they just want you to shut up. I know in my home that if I get a disrespectful outburst from my eldest daughter, it is normally because she is worried about something. I have observed her long enough to know that normally this is the case. So when it happens, I don't jump down her throat, I just leave her and later go to see her and ask if there is anything she would like to talk about, as she doesn't normally act this way. If she says No then that is fine, but this is about me recognising that there may be something beneath the surface, rather than a disrespectful outburst. So when your teenager behaves in this way ask:

Have I been clear about what disrespectful behaviour is?

Have I been consistent with pulling them up on this?

Could there be something else going on?

Help! It has all gone wrong!

Here, I am going to give you the final steps to the process above, where your child has sworn at you and you have asked them to stop, but they continue.

Step three – "You are still swearing at me, even though I ask you to stop. If you continue, I will walk away."

Step Four – Follow through.

As before, this may get worse before it gets better. Change is never pretty, but if we are clear and consistent and keep going, it will pay off. If you have a child who has a tendency to follow you around, then you may have to leave the house. This is not a punishment – "If you continue I will send you to your room, take away your phone, etc." It is a consequence that clearly links into what they are doing. "If you talk to me disrespectfully I will remove myself from the situation."

Extra Credit

If you really want to take this one deeper, it is a great one to play with.

Let's start with YOU.

Make a list of all the things you could do that would show that you respect yourself - big or small, whatever comes up, write it on the list. Then get your diary out, and each week plan to do one of the items you've listed. The next suggestion may seem a little strange, but it works – try it! Every day look in the mirror and say, "I respect me".

Look at your home and the day-to-day running of it and ask how, as a household, you might not be showing respect towards each other, for example, not knocking on doors before entering, etc. From the list, pick the top three changes that you think will make the biggest impact, and implement them.

If you are really brave, make a list of all the things you respect about your teen - I am talking about personal qualities, for example, determination. Then each day make it your mission to tell them what you respect or appreciate about them.

Week Three

How to work with your teen to instill responsibility.

Welcome to your third week in your programme. This week we will be working together to show you how to work with your teen to instil responsibility.

This chapter contains:

1. Your 3-minute daily emotional workout

2. Your 2-minute brain workout

3. Your 1-minute implementation exercise

4. Help! Why is my teenager acting this way? Background information and knowledge into why this may be happening and what you can do to ease the strain.

5. Help! It has all gone wrong! What to do if things don't quite go the way you planned.

6. Extra Credit – for those parents who are ultra brave and want to take it even further.

As always, it is up to you how you work through the chapter; there is no hard and fast rule, each person will work at their own pace and in their own manner. Take what resonates most for you from this lesson and start there.

The questions in each chapter are designed to allow you to self-coach yourself and will deepen the learning and experience for you.

How to work with your teen to instil responsibility

Responsibility is such a big word, and a word I am passionate about. I think that nowadays, our children don't take enough responsibility for themselves, their actions and their lives and frankly, why should they? As parents we do everything for them. What would make them want to? We have, I believe, set up a society that makes it OK for young people to duck out of their responsibilities. But no more; it is time to let go of the reins and show your 'little darling' what things are like in the real world!

As parents, it is so easy for us to take the simple way out of a situation and more often than not this involves stepping in and saving our children. We give them responsibilities and then we step in when they don't deliver, rather than working with them to come up with a solution because, yes, it is quicker and easier! However, the more we do that, the more our child will not show responsibility. Often, we give responsibility to our child and then step in because we don't trust them to deliver, or, even worse, we give them a responsibility and may not be clear on what that means or how it is to be delivered. Therefore they fail, so we end up proving ourselves right, that they are not responsible. It is a never-ending cycle.

To give responsibility is to give trust, and as parents we need to get clear what both these words means to us and our family, because responsibility and trust for one family might mean something entirely different to another. We also have to be willing to give responsibility and allow our children to fail, as that is the only way they learn.

Let me give you an example from my own life. I remember when my eldest daughter was 10 and she came to me and asked if she could choose her own bedtime. Like most parents I initially panicked and thought no, but I did what I always do when I don't know what to do and asked her to give me some time to think about it. I retired to my thinking chair and asked myself what did I really want for my child? The answer was that I wanted her to grow up responsible, resilient and ready for life. So was this a step in the right direction? Yes! So, I had decided it was certainly something that could allow her to show responsibility but really, how could I let a 10-year-old choose her own bedtime? I then asked what was I worried about, what did I think could go wrong? I thought that she would stay up until all hours, not get up for school, that we would have massive fights in the morning, that her school work would suffer and it would be a downward spiral. I also thought that Eddie and I would not get any time alone. So then I asked myself what I could put in place that would allow this not to happen. It was easy, I needed to put conditions around it and these were...

She needs to be out of the communal room at 9.00

She needs to get herself up for school and be ready to learn

Her grades should not suffer due to a lack of sleep.

If I had these, would I be happy for her to choose her own bedtime? The answer was yes.

What would I do if she proved herself irresponsible around this?

I would take her bedtime back for a week and I would be prepared to do this three times before I decided that she was not ready to do this for 6 months.

So we discussed this and I told her the conditions and the consequences should she prove irresponsible. Now, at 15, she hasn't broken this agreement. Once she puts herself to bed there is no struggle, no argument - and she gets herself up every morning. She is also doing well at school.

The questions I asked myself.

1. What do I want for my child, and is this a step in the right direction?

2. What am I worried about, what do I think could go wrong?

3. What will I do if she proves irresponsible around this?

We never know what our children are capable of until we give them a chance. We never know what they are able to do until we stop thinking what is right and what is wrong and start doing what feels right for us.

Your 3-minute emotional workout

For me, working on your emotional stuff is key to being a strong and powerful parent. However, it is not easy. When you are doing these emotional exercises, don't get too involved with what comes up. Just notice it and let it go. We have a tendency to 'navel gaze', feel sorry and think there is something wrong with us. We all have stuff – emotional baggage - and to move forward all we have to do is notice it and move on.

Firstly, I want you to find a quiet space where you will not be disturbed and take three deep breaths. This will just balance you.

Then I just want you to sit with these three questions. Just ask them of yourself and notice what comes up in terms of thoughts, feelings and emotions.

1. Where could you take responsibility for your own life more?

2. What stops you allowing your child to take responsibility?

3. What was the message I got about respect as a child?

4. How did you show responsibility as a child?

If you get nothing then that is fine too; just come back to it another day.

Just sit for three minutes and after that have a notebook to hand and quickly jot down the thoughts, feelings or emotions that come up for you.

Your two minute thinking exercise.

I say 'thinking', but I am going to be asking you to write too.

Getting all the feelings out to do with a situation will really support you in moving forward.

Get a pen and paper and the pad you used to jot down your observations from the above exercise.

Then just answer these questions on the paper; write as much or as little as you feel.

1. What was the one thought, feeling or emotion stuck in my mind from the previous exercise?

2. What makes this so poignant for me?

3. How is it impacting my relationship with my child now?

Then just sit, take a few breaths and release.

Your implementation exercise.

OK, now I want you to pick one daily responsibility, something relatively 'everyday', something that you want your child to own. It should be something that doesn't feel too frightening for either of you! Once you decide on the responsibility, go through this system.

Step One: Get clear how this will allow your child to be more responsible

Step Two: Write a list of all the things you are worried about should you give your child responsibility for this, all the things that might go wrong.

Step Three: Look at the list and ask yourself what conditions you can put in place to ensure that things don't go wrong (as I did with the bedtime).

Step Four: Think of what the consequences will be if conditions are not met. These are not punishments, they are natural consequences, things that link into what has gone wrong.

Now you are going to give them the responsibility! In the case of my daughter it would have looked like this.

"Bronte, I want you to take responsibility for your bedtime. I am happy for you to do this as long as you are out of the communal room by 9.00, you get yourself up for school, you are ready to learn and your school work doesn't suffer. If these conditions don't occur, I will take your bedtime back for a week. I am willing to do this on three occasions; it it's still not working after that I will take the responsibility back for 6 months, as it will have shown me that you are not ready for this responsibility yet."

Can you see how clear this is and how everyone knows clearly what is expected of them? That is how clear you need to be. You can also, for added effect, add the words, "I trust you".

Help! Why is my teenager acting this way?

Responsibility isn't something that we just wake up one day and decide to do; it is something that is learned and quite often is learnt through making mistakes and getting it wrong. Just because your child has reached the teen years doesn't mean they are suddenly responsible or know how to be. You need to teach them this. If we look back to the information about brain development we find big clues here as to why teenagers make so many mistakes and get it wrong so often. The frontal lobe which is highly affected in the teen years prunes itself like a tree, it gets rids of branches (connections) and decides which to re grow. Most of these connections are to do with understanding logical consequences. So when something seems clearly obvious to us, it may not be so to them. Things we think they may know they actually may not know at all. So we need to spell things out, almost like we did in the toddler years. We need to do the 'Responsibility for Dummies' version!

Help! It has all gone wrong!

Firstly, when it all goes wrong I encourage you to look at the system (the process you used to set the agreement up). I don't think people fail; I think systems fail. So, first, were you clear enough? For example, in my case, if I had not explained myself clearly, Bronte might have thought that the bedtime situation didn't apply to weekends. Tweak the system first, if you think it needs tweaking, and then start again. If you think it is not a system error but it was, in fact, just a case of your child being disobedient, then you need to follow through on what you said you would do. So, in the previous example, I made it I clear that I would just take the bedtime back if conditions were not met. However, in some cases the parameters will not be clear, because of a situation that could not be anticipated or planned for. For example, one of my client's sons took the car without permission and crashed it – this is not something that my client could have foreseen at all, as he wasn't even old enough to drive.

It is important that you don't jump in and make a rash punishment. First, give yourself time to think.

"Johnny, I am disappointed in you. I trusted you and you have broken my trust. I need time to think about how I am doing to handle this and I suggest that you also think about what we are going to do. Let's give ourselves 24 hours and then discuss it."

In the 24 hours, think about what you want to do, something that links into the crime, so to speak. In this case, the parent decided that when he could drive she would not put him on her insurance for 2 years and the car he had been promised would not be purchased until 2 years later. She also decided that his allowance would go to pay for the damage to the car.

When they sat down she first asked him what he thought. He thought that he should pay for the damage and then she told him what she thought and while he didn't like it, he agreed.

The lesson was learnt – and will continue to be, as long as she keeps true to her word. In a case like this, consistency gains both respect and results.

Extra Credit

Responsibility is a huge area of our self-fulfilment and I really want you to delve into your own life here.

Get a big piece of paper and on it write the headings:

- Relationships

- Finances

- Career/Business

- Health

- Family and Friends

- Personal Growth

- Fun and recreation

- Environment

On each, score out of 10 how much responsibility you take for each of these areas in your life and one thing that you could do to take more responsibility

You will end up with 8 areas, duly assessed.

Then each week pick one area and see how you could raise your own self-imposed score.

Once you start to take more responsibility for your own life, so will your child for theirs.

Week Four

How to stop nagging and give your teen empowering choices.

Welcome to your fourth week in your programme. This week we will be working together to help you stop nagging and give your teen empowering choices.

This chapter contains:

1. Your 3-minute daily emotional workout

2. Your 2-minute brain workout

3. Your 1-minute implementation exercise

4. Help! Why is my teenager acting this way? Background information and knowledge into why this may be happening and what you can do to ease the strain.

5. Help! It has all gone wrong! What to do if things don't quite go the way you planned.

6. Extra Credit – for those parents who are ultra brave and want to take it even further.

As always, it is up to you how you work through the chapter, there is no hard and fast rule; each person will work at their own pace and in their own manner. Take what resonates most for you from this lesson and start there.

The questions in each chapter are designed to allow you to self-coach and will deepen the learning and experience for you.

Stop nagging and give your teen empowering choices

nag•ging adjective

1. Continually faultfinding, complaining, or petulant: a nagging parent.

2. Persistently recurring; unrelenting: a nagging backache.

If you are anything like me, then you might find yourself nagging constantly and wondering where you went wrong. I sometimes catch myself nagging, almost wondering who it is talking, and then realising that it's me! Some days can often feel like an absolute 'nag-fest' and I begin to even bore myself. Do you recognise any of this? What I have found in my own home and in the homes of my clients is that nagging is one of the easiest things to conquer, so that's the good news! The bad news is that you need to put in a bit of effort…. Nagging generally happens for a few reasons; because we just have not got a system that does what the nagging does for us, or we just don't trust our teens enough.

We expect our children and teens to know what we are thinking, but often we haven't even told them what we want or what is required.

Let's deal with the system bit first, because I do think this is the easiest to deal with. Families are very complicated units; we have multiple people with multiple agendas, all sharing the same space and trying to make life work. And things get complicated, missed and forgotten. To deal with this you need some kind of great planning system, either something on-line, a calendar, a diary or even a blackboard or large piece of paper. What I suggest all families do is this: on Sunday, have a quick family meeting where you all come together, look at the week ahead and see where support may be needed for each other.

If we are always nagging because we don't trust our children, then we need to deal with that in another way. If you remember, when we looked at the different types of parenting, we talked about moving from manager to coach and saw that when a child gets abstract thought that suddenly your gentle reminders may be met with much resistance. They don't need you to manage anymore, but they do need you to support them to learn how to manage themselves. And that is where we often lose it; we manage them, stop managing them and then expect them to be able to do it. However, it doesn't work that way, they need to learn how!

As parents, we have to walk them though the processes of managing themselves, letting them make their own mistakes and tweaking their own systems (I will give you the system for doing this later). For example, 'ready for school' in our language may mean something entirely different to them. If a system won't do the job and no amount of trying will change them, you may have to do the really hard thing and step back. I have coached lots of parents to do this around college decisions and getting jobs with much satisfaction, but there is a way of doing it.

Let's say you are trying to get them to make a decision about which college to go to, trying your best to get them interested and motivated, but they are not making any moves in the right direction. Here is what you need to do:

"Jenny, I really want to support you with your college decision, but I am no longer willing to argue and nag about it, so I am handing it over to you. It is your responsibility and I trust you to make the right decisions."

That is the first part; make sure you hand over responsibility and tell them you trust them to make the right decisions.

Then you need to tell them what you will and will not do.

So in this example...

"I will support you as much as you want, but only when you ask me and only with enough notice. I will not nag you about it, remind you of the deadlines (unless you want me to) or organise any visits. You need to do this. Also, if you don't get your application in on time I will not intervene on your behalf and if you don't go to college, I expect you to get a job or be in another form of education by September".

You need to make it crystal clear what you will and will not do, and you need to be able to follow though and be strong enough to trust, assuring them that even if it all goes wrong it will still all be OK. Sometimes to learn, they need to trip up.

My daughter recently was studying for a mock exam. I could see what she was doing wasn't working and I attempted to help her, without much luck. I eventually told her that it was her responsibility and I was leaving it to her to figure out the best way. If her way worked I would leave her alone; however, if the mock result was bad I would step in. She got an E in the mock, so I stepped in. But there was still only so much I could do and she had to take responsibility. If she chose not to, then I had to be OK with that. She might have to suffer the consequences of failing - which is a powerful lesson.

Your 3-minute emotional workout

For me, working on your emotional stuff is key to being a strong and powerful parent. However, it is not easy. When you are doing these emotional exercises, don't get too involved with what comes up. Just notice it and let it go. We have a tendency to 'navel gaze', feel sorry and think there is something wrong with us. We all have stuff – emotional baggage - and to move forward all we have to do is notice it and move on.

Firstly, I want you to find a quiet space where you will not be disturbed and take three deep breaths. This will just balance you.

Then I just want you to sit with these questions. Just ask them of yourself and notice what comes up in terms of thoughts, feelings and emotions.

1. How were you given choices in your life?

2. How did you feel about failure?

3. What is your fear for your child if they fail?

4. Is that a realistic feeling?

If you get nothing come up, then that is fine; just come back to it another day.

Just sit for three minutes and after that, have a notebook to hand and quickly jot down the thoughts, feelings or emotions that comes up for you.

Your two minute thinking exercise.

I say 'thinking', but I am going to be asking you to write too.

Getting all the feelings out to do with a situation will really support you in moving forward.

Get a pen and paper and the pad you used to jot down your observations from the above exercise.

Then just answer these questions on the paper; write as much or as little as you feel.

1. What was the one thought, feeling or emotion stuck in my mind from the previous exercise?

2. What makes this so poignant for me?

3. How is it impacting my relationship with my child now?

Then just sit, take a few breaths and release.

Your implementation exercise.

Plan and run one family meeting. I have guidelines for you, but run it however you feel will work best for you.

Give you child a choice in something that you are currently far too involved in, using the method I outlined above.

How to Implement Your Family Meetings.

1) Announce that you would like to have family meetings once per week. Your children are not going to meet this request with joy, so I suggest that you approach it like this.

"I am sick of all the arguing and nagging going on, how everything is getting left to the last minute and we are missing things or being late. I want this to stop. Each week, I want us to sit down and quickly go over the week ahead so that we all know what is happening and there are no nasty surprises. When do you think will be a good time for this meeting and do you have any suggestions on how we do it?"

2) Lock in a time and structure. Let you child know that you don't want this to interfere with their life or schoolwork, so get them to suggest a time. I find Sundays after lunch tend to work well.

3) Regular structure. Set an agenda so everyone knows what to expect and what he or she needs to bring to the meeting. Also, set a time limit so that everyone knows that it will last 15 minutes, for example.

At the meeting, have the calendar or system that you use as a family

I find going through these things is a very productive way of moving forward.

- Any events/appointments coming up that week outside the norm

- Anything happening that anyone requires help with, including homework assignments, lifts, etc.

- Something that may happen that the rest of the family needs to be aware of.

- Anything great that happened last week that someone may want to share.

Then add things to the family calendar as required, so everyone is aware. What I then like to do is do a monthly review of the previous month. I use these four questions below to help me:

1. What do you want to change?

2. What do you want to continue?

3. What do you want to stop doing?

4. What do you want to start doing

We each write the answer to these questions on a post-it note and going from there, we discuss, challenge and plan a way forward. It is a great way of not making anyone wrong.

Help! Why is my teenager acting this way?

I think that during the teenage years, a lot of our own fears can be brought to the forefront by our teenagers. These are called narcissistic injuries, and we can often want to protect them from all the mistakes we made or all the things that went wrong in our own lives. However if we think about it, what went wrong and the failures we made in our lives are what shaped us. Our failures are what enable us to learn and move forward. So, our protective instincts for our children can actually mean that we limit and stunt that personal development and growth. When we constantly step in and nag, it gives a message to our children that we don't trust them, and often we don't. When we trust them and they grow up, they don't need us so much and for some of us that can be scary. The dependency that has been there for so long is no longer required.

Help! It has all gone wrong!

I am such a fan of choice, what it promotes and the results it generates. As adults we are faced with choices every day, yet quite often we do not allow our children the same privilege, telling them where and when they must do something in our efforts to control them. Recently, I was working with a twelve-year-old who was refusing to go to school and had not been for seven months. Her family, very concerned, just kept telling her that she had to go and the more they told her, the more she dug her heels in. I asked her what her choices were in this situation; she stated that staying at home was her only choice. I then asked her what other choices there were and together we came up with a list of four other choices - on-line school, home tutors, going back to her old school or picking a new school. She initially opted for the on-line school and within a week we had her learning again. Every time she asked me what I thought she should do, I just told her that the choice was hers and that I trusted her to do what was right. After a month she said she was ready to go back to her old school and I have been told that as of today, she has successfully spent a week at school.

The point is that it was a choice that she came to by herself; by taking the pressure off and putting the choice back onto her, she did what was right. When you are struggling with one of your teenager's issues, go through the choices with them, tell them the choice is theirs and you trust them to do what is right. Then watch them squirm. They find this concept so difficult, since they are so used to being told what to do and having something to fight against. They are not sure what to do and most will eventually make a good choice. You just need to get off their back and allow them the time.

There are a few other ways you can use this tool. Instead of saying, "Tom, go and do the washing up now!" you can say, "Tom, you can do the washing up now or after this TV programme, which do you choose?" You are giving him choice but also making sure that what needs to be done gets done.

You can also use the 'Choice and State' technique.

One of my clients was finding herself nagging and nagging about the laundry. Lyn would say, "Alan, I am about to do the laundry. Can you bring your dirty clothes down?" He would say something like "I can't be bothered," or "I'm sleeping" and she would simply say, "You have a choice Alan, I will not be coming up to get it and I will not be doing any more washing until Thursday." Lyn had stuck to her word and had not gone up to get the laundry and, needless to say, Alan did not want to wear something that was dirty. He came down all ablaze asking her why she had not washed his favourite shirt. She explained that she had told him to bring his dirty clothes down and, as he had chosen not to, the washing had not been done. Alan was less than happy and blew up, swearing and shouting and ranting and raving, telling her to wash the shirt now. She refused, so he pushed her and ran out of the house to his friends. Lyn rang me in tears, needing some support.

The first thing I asked her was, "What do you want to do?" Here was her first dilemma. She wanted to wash the shirt to make everything better but she knew that if she did, she was giving in and throwing away the good work she had done. She was here, after all, to teach Alan responsibility, understanding and independence and if she gave in, how would she be true to herself?

What would you do? Would you have washed the shirt?

Here was an important choice for Lyn, between help and rescue. She could take the easy and soft option by washing the shirt and rescuing him, or she could help him, which may take a little longer but would teach him more in the long run. It's so easy when we are busy, tired and drained to just rescue our children and give in. But what are they learning if we do that? When we choose rescue, we are denying our teenagers a valuable learning process. As parents we are leaders (of our children) and as leaders we must stop doing what is easy in our lives and start doing what is right.

The 'choice and state' technique

Step 1 — State the behaviour and tell them what they are doing.

"Alan, do you realise you are shouting at me about something that is not my fault? I want to help you but I cannot talk to you while you are shouting at me. If you stop then we can discuss it, but if you continue then I will walk away."

Step 2 — Show understanding

"I appreciate how important this is to you and that you want the shirt now."

Step 3 — Explain the situation

"The reason the shirt is not washed is because you did not bring it to me when I asked, and this is the result of your choice."

Step 4 — State what you will and will not do

"I can see how important this is to you but I am not prepared to wash it for you. However, I will show you how to use the washing machine."

'Laundry hell' ended with Lyn showing Alan how to use the machine and he was never late again when he was asked to bring his washing.

Whenever you are in any conflict with your teenager, think how you can give them a choice that will also get done what needs to be done. Just think what a valuable life lesson you are teaching them.

Extra Credit

Get a pen and paper and just write, uninterrupted for 5 minutes, around these questions. Don't censor what you write just write.

1. Am I afraid at all about giving my child more choice?

2. What frightens me about giving them more choice?

3. Who did I need to be able to become to give them more choice?

4. Who did I need to be able to become to give them more choice?

Week Five

How to remove any tension and ensure that everyone is getting along better.

Welcome to your fifth week in your programme. This week we will be working together to remove any tensions and ensure that everyone is getting along better.

This chapter contains:

1. Your 3-minute daily emotional workout

2. Your 2-minute brain workout

3. Your 1-minute implementation exercise

4. Help! Why is my teenager acting this way? Background information and knowledge into why this may be happening and what you can do to ease the strain.

5. Help! It has all gone wrong! What to do if things don't quite go the way you planned.

6. Extra Credit – for those parents who are ultra brave and want to take it even further.

As always, it is up to you how you work through the chapter, there is no hard and fast rule; each person will work at their own pace and in their own manner. Take what resonates most for you from this lesson and start there.

The questions in each chapter are designed to allow you to self-coach and will deepen the learning and experience for you.

How to remove any tension and ensure that everyone is getting along better.

Tension, arguments, bickering and fighting are commonplace in most homes and I think when we have different characters and people living together under one roof, it is bound to happen. While we can live harmonious lives and in relative peace, I am not sure we can have that all the time and actually, wouldn't it be really boring? What happens in most homes is that parents are scared of conflict and at the first sign of it they try and diffuse the situations, taking on responsibility for everyone's happiness in the home. This is a ridiculous thing to do and really unattainable.

The only person that we can make happy is our self, and the only person that we can control is our self. We can't control someone else's reaction to something, only our own reaction to what is happening.
The key in any household is recognising the signs that things may be heating up and taking appropriate action at that point.

If you imagine anger as a temperature gauge, with 0 representing calm and 10 representing fully flowing anger, it is very hard to bring a person down from level 10. The trick comes in recognising all the points between 1-10 and what you need to do to stop the temperature gauge rising anymore.

Let me take my eldest daughter for example; she is very emotional and can 'lose it' quite easily, but by watching her I am able to see her process. When she is getting mad she will first ignore you, and then if you persist she will ask you to stop, in a snappy sort of manner. If I continue to press her she will shout, and if I go past that point – well, welcome to Level 10! By watching her, I know that after she asks me to stop, if I leave her alone she can bring herself down, but if I carry on it takes hours for her to calm down. As a parent I know that if I get a snappy 'Stop It!' or 'Leave It Alone!', then I need to do that and I know that, after an hour, if I go in to talk to her she will have calmed down and we will be able to talk about it sensibly. If I push her however, knowing what I know, then really I have only got myself to blame. I am also able to tell her Dad and sister how to deal with her when she is like this.

When we understand someone's anger process we are able to back off rather than aggravating the situation. We are also able to support them in learning how to handle the situation themselves.

It is always a really good idea to talk through volatile situations after asking your teen what they thought they could have done, how perhaps they could have got their anger out in a constructive way that doesn't hurt anyone (or their feelings), and what you can do to help them. Some families I work with have produced code words to use that remind everyone involved what they need to do in this situation. Getting rid of the tension is partly down to acknowledging that conflict will happen and knowing what to do with it when it does.

I think is it also partly down to understanding that what each of us want or need is different. We all have different levels of need within a family and often, if we don't understand this, we can make ourselves wrong for someone else not behaving in a certain way.

In the work in which I am trained, I identify the human condition's five basic needs. These are:

- Survival

- Love and belonging

- Power (self power, rather than power over others)

- Fun

- Freedom

Let me show you how these pan out with me and the relationships within my family. I have a strong need for power, fun and freedom and a lesser need for love and belonging. In the relationship with my husband we are well balanced; his need for power is not as strong as mine so I can lead most things. His need for freedom is about medium which balances out my high and keeps us grounded. His need for fun is equal to mine; his need for love and belonging is higher than mine and this could cause problems, which I have explained to him. He could easily interpret my lack of wanting cuddles and always being with him as not loving him, which is not true; it is just that this isn't as important for me as it is for him. Both of my children have strong needs for love and belonging so they know to turn to Eddie more for emotional comfort, whereas if they want a hug from me it is best to ask, as I don't really give them voluntarily. Both my daughters a have strong need for fun which means that we can really have a great time together. One of them has a strong need for power, the other low. As for freedom, the same; one high, one very low. We could, left to our own devices, have many fights and rarely get along, but since the whole family understands this information it allows us to make sense more of what is happening. It allows us not to think another is 'wrong' for being the way they are, and understand that what they need is different to what we our self might need.

Most conflicts occur because someone's needs are not met, so they are doing what they can to meet them.

That is all we can ever do, behave to meet our needs. So a child with a high need for freedom will constantly break curfews, because a curfew feels like you are hemming them in. A child with a low need for love and belonging can make a parent with a high need feel like they don't care. When we start to use this within our home it instils a great sense of understanding and allows us to form a better understanding with that individual child. My child with a low need for freedom asks for curfews and will always be home early, my child with the high need will push them, so I allow them to be a bit looser with room for movement, as I know if I hem her in she will rebel.

We make things so difficult for ourselves as parents, believing that we must treat every child the same and in line with some imaginary rule book. When we realise that people behave to meet their needs, it makes things so much easier.

Your 3-minute emotional workout

For me, working on your emotional stuff is key to being a strong and powerful parent. However it is not easy. When you are doing these emotional exercises don't get too involved with what comes up. Just notice it and let it go. We have a tendency to 'navel gaze', feel sorry and think there is something wrong with us. We all have stuff – emotional baggage - and to move forward all we have to do is notice it and move on.

First, I want you to find a quiet space where you will not be disturbed and take three deep breaths. This will just balance you.

Then I just want you to sit with these three questions. Just ask them of yourself and notice what comes up in terms of thoughts, feelings and emotions.

1. What makes me angry?

2. Where do I feel anger in my body?

3. How could I realise my anger in a positive way?

If you get nothing come up, that is fine. Just come back to it another day.

Just sit for three minutes and after that have a notebook to hand and quickly jot down the thoughts, feelings or emotions that come up for you.

Your two minute thinking exercise.

I say 'thinking', but I am going to be asking you to write too.

Getting all the feelings out to do with a situation will really support you in moving forward.

Get a pen and paper and the pad you used to jot down your observations from the above exercise.

Then just answer these questions on the paper; write as much or as little as you feel.

1. What was the one thought, feeling or emotion stuck in my mind from the previous exercise?

2. What makes this so poignant for me?

3. How is it impacting my relationship with my child now?

Then just sit, take a few breaths and release.

Your implementation exercise.

Discuss the anger thermometer with your child and go through it with them if you can. If you can, observe them when they are angry, make a mental note of what happens and think of when you need to back off.

Help! Why is my teenager acting this way?

The teenage years is a time that is full of emotions, new feelings, new awakenings and new stirrings that for most can be pretty scary. Teens feel things they can't make sense of, say things they don't understand and go into moods for reasons beyond their control. It is a difficult, introspective time for most and making sense of it all can leave most tired, frustrated and irritable. Is it no surprise that they fly off the handle at the slightest thing and we reprimand them for this? They are making some of the biggest decisions they will ever make and they are making them with a confused mind. As we have mentioned previously, part of their job is to test the system and part of this will be testing their relationships with their family and seeing how much they can push them. Also, their dopamine levels decrease, meaning that they need more of everything to stimulate them and for some, this can mean more intense arguing. It is not that they argue more in the teen years it is just that these arguments become more intense.

Help! It has all gone wrong!

We all lose it, we all go too far, and often you or your teen will 'lose it'. Make it clear what is and is not acceptable around you or in your home, and use the process we went through in the saying No and instilling responsibility chapters. Always say sorry if you feel that you could have handled the situation better. If you can, always talk about the outburst afterwards, knowing that you may need to tweak a lot of things a lot of times before you are running on more of an even keel.

Extra Credit

Really delve into the basic needs using the information below.

William Glasser, in his 'Control Theory' (later renamed to 'Choice Theory') detailed five needs.

These needs are:

Survival (food, clothing, shelter, breathing, personal safety and others)

And four fundamental psychological needs:

Belonging/connecting/love

Power/significance/competence

Freedom/autonomy

Fun/learning

In this exercise we are going to look at the four psychological needs in few different ways.

1. You will look at these needs as they relate to yourself and your own personal development.

2. You will try and establish the need levels of your partner/spouse and your children.

3. You are going to identify where these differences in needs may cause challenges.

4. You will think about what solutions you can put in place to ensure that your family understand this concept more.

Your Needs

Love/Belonging. How important is this need to you? (Use the scoring system of 1-10 - 1 low, 10 high) How much is this need met in your life? How can you get this need met more? How is this need impacting your family?

Power. How important is this need to you? (Use the scoring system of 1-10 - 1 low, 10 high) How much is this need met in your life? How can you get this need met more? How is this need impacting your family?

Freedom. How important is this need to you? (Use the scoring system of 1-10 - 1 low, 10 high) How much is this need met in your life? How can you get this need met more? How is this need impacting your family?

Fun. How important is this need to you? (Use the scoring system of 1-10 - 1 low, 10 high) How much is this need met in your life? How can you get this need met more? How is this need impacting your family?

Your Family's Needs

Score each family member on how high you think their need is for each need listed.

Need	Member 1	Member 2	Member 3	Member 4
Love/Belonging				
Fun				
Freedom				
Power				

1. How do you think these differences in needs could cause challenges?

2. What solutions can you put in place to counteract what you have written above?

Week Six

How to talk to your teen so they will listen and listen so they will talk.

Welcome to your sixth week in your programme . This chapter we will be working together to show you how to talk to your teen so that they will listen, and listen so that they will talk.

This chapter contains:

1. Your 3-minute daily emotional workout

2. Your 2-minute brain workout

3. Your 1-minute implementation exercise

4. Help! Why is my teenager acting this way? Background information and knowledge into why this may be happening and what you can do to ease the strain.

5. Help! It has all gone wrong! What to do if things don't quite go the way you planned.

6. Extra Credit – for those parents who are ultra brave and want to take it even further.

As always, it is up to you how you work through the chapter; there are no hard and fast rules, each person will work at their own paces and in their own manner. Take what resonates most for you from this lesson and start there first.

The questions in each module are designed to allow you to self-coach and will deepen the learning and experience for you.

How to talk to your teen so that they will listen, and listen so that they will talk.

Communication is the cornerstone of everything; if we can talk and continue talking, then we can get through the teen years relatively unscathed, in my experience. However, it is also the thing that seems to fall apart the easiest and quickest. Time gets in the way, we receive little communication apart from grunts; teens are notoriously good at cutting us off, but we shouldn't let that get in the way or stop us from trying. If you look up the word communication in the dictionary, just to give us a starting point, it states . . .

"The activity of conveying information. A connection allowing access. Allows people to exchange thoughts by one of several methods." A few key things came up for me here.

Active - to me, active means that we are engaged and fully present, making a decision to communicate.

Connection - it comes from a centre, a place of heart and its aim is to connect with the other person.

Exchange - it is two way! Yes, I hate to say it - they need to speak too, and you need to listen.

So, if we look at communication as being an active, exchanging connection, then the whole picture changes, doesn't it? Most communication with our children is merely us telling them what to do, has no real connection and is anything but active and purposeful. I believe that by changing the communication patterns in your home, they can change your relationships, dissipate conflict and make your home more harmonious.

Communication is the glue that holds families together, yet we seem to be pretty bad and ineffective at it. Communication in most homes seems to consist of instructional (do this, do that), logistical arrangements or informational (getting information from your children). Hardly any time is spent in real conversation, conversation where we bond; get to know our children, learn about their ideas, how they feel and what their innermost thoughts are.

Most families when asked will say that they spend lot of time with their children, but on deeper reflection most of this time is spent watching TV; it is being in the same room together rather than really being together. The same goes for conversation; people will say that their families talk a lot, but do they have real conversations, or talk just for the sake of talking? Just by changing your communication patterns you can improve any situation. You can do this by:

Inserting talking moments into their everyday routine

Finding systems and structure to eliminate the need for conversations that are instructional and logistical

Finding ways for the family to spend time together

What is a family talking moment?

Talking moments are simply snippets of time in your day where you have an honest, open conversation with your children. A conversation that really has no purpose, is not aimed at getting them to do something, but instead is aimed at deepening your understanding of your child and your relationship with them. These moments don't have to be complicated and I highly recommend you make them as simple as possible; snippets of time in your daily routine, not a time out, let's have a chat sort of thing. Here are some suggestions of how you can inject talking moments into your daily routine.

I think there are three key moments in the average family's day:

The school run – I don't mean the manic getting out the house, I mean once you are in the car driving. You have a captive audience, so make use of it.

The evening meal – I believe that the family getting together and having a meal is essential at least three times a week. It is valuable bonding and communication time. You can use these moments to talk in general or start conversations about items in the news or of interest to the whole family, like your next family holiday.

While watching soaps or TV programme – I think this is a great idea as so many issues are raised in soaps that can spur a conversation afterwards. Wait until the programme has finished and ask them what they thought about a topic raised.

Your 3-minute emotional workout

For me, working on your emotional stuff is key to being a strong and powerful parent. However it is not easy. When you are doing these emotional exercises don't get too involved with what comes up. Just notice it and let it go. We have a tendency to 'navel gaze', feel sorry and think there is something wrong with us. We all have stuff – emotional baggage - and to move forward all we have to do is notice it and move on.

First, I want you to find a quiet space where you will not be disturbed and take three deep breaths. This will just balance you.

Then I just want you to sit with these three questions. Just ask them of yourself and notice what comes up in terms of thoughts, feelings and emotions.

1. How did your family communicate when you were a child?

2. How do you think this has impacted your communication style?

3. If you asked your children how you communicated, what would they say?

If you get nothing come up, that is fine. Just come back to it another day.

Just sit for three minutes and after that have a notebook to hand and quickly jot down the thoughts, feelings or emotions that come up for you.

Your two minute thinking exercise.

I say 'thinking', but I am going to be asking you to write too.

Getting all the feelings out to do with a situation will really support you in moving forward.

Get a pen and paper and the pad you used to jot down your observations from the above exercise.

Then just answer these questions on the paper; write as much or as little as you feel.

1. What was the one thought, feeling or emotion stuck in my mind from the previous exercise?

2. What makes this so poignant for me?

3. How is it impacting my relationship with my child now?

Then just sit, take a few breaths and release.

Your implementation exercise.

I want you to look at your daily activities and see where you can insert a talking moment and then just start the conversation.

Help! Why is my teenager acting this way?

Communication breaks down for all sorts of reasons. Firstly, as we have discussed many times it is part of the teenager's job to challenge the system so they can find balance. It is only through this challenge that they are able to understand who they are or want to be as an adult.

Secondly, their abstract thought starts to develop, which has them question things like they never have before and the things that they are most likely to question first are their parents. This new abstract thought can leave them very confused and really just wanting to be left alone, so their lack of communication could be because they simply are trying to work things out in their head. Their relations with their friends get more complicated, school puts on more pressure, they start thinking about love relationships and they feel pushed between wanting to grow up and wanting to be looked after. It is a very difficult and challenging time. Also, their temporal lobe in their brain is affected by all the changes that are happening and the temporal lobe governs language, so it is no surprise that paragraphs turn to grunts and they seem to develop a whole language of their own. Also teenagers, particularly boys, are designed to move away from their parents particularly their mother; it is part of what nature intends.

Help! It has all gone wrong!

What do I do when my child will not talk to me?

Do your conversations go something like,

Parent: Can we have a chat?

Child: No I don't want to chat – get out of my room. I don't want to talk to you!

Parent walks away…..

This can be a real challenge for any parent.

What do you do when your child will not talk to you?

Here are a few tips.

1. Don't give up – just because they don't want to talk to you, it does not mean forever, it just means for now so don't give up forever, ask them to let you know when it is OK.

2. The 'can we have a chat' line is normally interpreted by a kid as 'you have done something wrong and we need to talk about it'! 'Can we have a chat' is, to us, often just this: I have an agenda to this conversation but I am trying to fool you by making you think I want a chat.

Children are not fools, they know they are about to get lectured, so why should they stick around? So instead of can we have a chat, use all the opportunities you have to talk outside of the dreaded 'can we have a chat'. Driving in the car, over the breakfast table, moments that are natural, where conversation can flow a little more easily.

3. A chat to a child normally means you talking, so instead of thinking of having a chat, think of having a listen instead. Zip your lips when you want to step in and if you listen, they will talk more.

Parents who have used this system do get to have a great chats with their children. When I asked one recently what she did differently here is what she said. She:

- Capitalized on him being open to talk, (i.e., making hay whilst the sun shines!).

- Showed interest and listened.

- Didn't bring up subjects he didn't want to talk about, or dropped them when he said he didn't want to talk about stuff.

- Praised him.

- Told him she appreciated the chat; he said the same.

- Was very grateful.

A system I really love around communication is the non-violent communication system. I suggest you get the book, I have put a small précis below for you .

Nonviolent Communication

Nonviolent Communication (NVC) is a process developed by Marshall Rosenberg. It is a way to communicate with greater compassion and clarity. It focuses on two things: honest self-expression — exposing what matters to oneself in a way that's likely to inspire compassion in others, and empathy — listening with deep compassion.

NVC postulates that conflict between individuals or groups is a result of miscommunication about these needs, often because of coercive language or manipulative language (e.g., inducing fear, guilt, shame, praise, blame, duty, obligation, punishment, or reward).One aim of NVC is to create a situation in which everyone's needs are met.

NVC advocates that in order to understand each other, the parties express themselves in objective and neutral terms (talking about their factual observations, feelings and needs) rather than in judgmental terms (such as good versus bad, right versus wrong, or fair versus unfair).

Definition

One definition of nonviolent communication offered by Rosenberg is the following:

Nonviolent Communication (NVC) is a way of speaking that facilitates the flow of communication needed to exchange information and resolve differences peacefully. It helps us identify our shared needs, encourages us to use language that increases goodwill, and avoid language that contributes to resentment or lowers self-esteem. Nonviolent Communication focuses our attention on compassion as our motivation, rather than fear, guilt, blame, or shame. It emphasizes taking personal responsibility for our choices and improving the quality of our relationships as our goal. It is effective even when the other person or group is not familiar with the process.

Process

NVC follows what is called the **OFNR process model**

The NVC model has three or four steps depending on the mode of use.

1. Observation

2. Feelings

3. Needs

4. Request

So how can you use these tips in your home?

So let's say that Tommy continues to come home and leave his school bag in the hallway. Using this model you would say

1. **Observe**

   "Tommy, I notice you have left your school bag in the hallway."

2. **Feelings**

   "When you do that it makes me feel that what I want is not important."

3. **Need**

   "When I come home from work I need the house to be ordered and tidy."

4. **Request**

   "Please remove your school bag."

Or let's say that Tommy was shouting at his mum.

1. **Observe**

   "Tommy, do you realise that you are shouting at your mum?"

2. **Feelings**

   "When you shout it makes me feel sad and a little angry."

3. **Need**

    "What I need is that we show respect in this house and don't shout."

4. **Request**

    "Please stop shouting."

Extra Credit

Look at the conversation in your home, examine it for a week and plot your results.

Your Families Communication patterns

For a week, I want you to track your homes communication patterns. All you need to do is quickly, at the end of the day, sit down with this document and think over all the conversations you have had. Note down the amount in time or percentage of how much of your communication time was spent on that area.

Instructional communication

Day One

Day Two

Day Three

Day Four

Day Five

Logistical/arrangement communication

Day One

Day Two

Day Three

Day Four

Day Five

Informational communication

Day One

Day Two

Day Three

Day Four

Day Five

Real conversation

Day One

Day Two

Day Three

Day Four

Day Five

After plotting this for a week, take a look at the results and answer these questions.

1. How much of your time was spent on real conversation?

2. What, if anything, has shocked you about these results?

3. What is the one thing you want to change?

4. What are you going to put in place to change that?

Switching your communication style

If you are really brave, you can delve even deeper and look at switching your communication pattern from a retributive to a restorative pattern. It is so easy for us to get stuck.

So let's look below at the old and new communication paradigms.

Old retributive communication styles

1. We talk about a child breaking the rules and think about punishment. We see it as a challenge to our authority. "You came in late and broke your curfew . . . you are grounded!"

2. We focus on establishing guilt and apportioning blame. "Did you do that to your sister? You should know better. You need to grow up!"

3. We see ourselves in a battle with our teenager/child for power and we believe our job is to impose some kind of unpleasantness to get that person to do what we want. "You never do what I say and help when I ask ... I am going to stop your allowance!"

4. We focus our attention on the right rules, adherence and process to get our child to conform.

5. We see their taking accountability as a loss or a punishment.

New Restorative communication styles

1. We see the misdemeanour as causing harm, not challenging us as an individual. We focus on the child taking accountability, which is defined as them understanding the impact of their action. "When you come in late I feel as if what we want is not important. How are we going to put this right?"

2. We focus on problem solving. "OK, we both live in the same house here and we need to get along. How can we do that and make sure we all get what we need?"

3. We focus on dialogue and everyone is involved and gets a say. We focus on reconciliation. "We do not share responsibilities fairly in this house. We need to sit down as a family and discuss how we can make this work for everyone."

4. We place our attention on the relationship. Our desired result is to focus on the relationship, not harm it.

5. We see accountability as a consequence of a choice and work with the child to make different choices.

I imagine that as some of you read this it is not easy to hear, maybe it goes against what you think is right, perhaps your relationship with your teenager is not even in a place where this is possible yet. Whatever is going through your head is fine; most of what I teach is against the norm. However, from working in some of the most challenging situations, I know this stuff works and I know it turns around relationships and very difficult children! See how you can switch your communication style this week.

Week Seven

How to punish and be tough without destroying the relationship.

Welcome to your seventh week in your programme. This week we will be working together to show you How to punish and be tough without destroying the relationship.

This chapter contains:

1. Your 3-minute daily emotional workout

2. Your 2-minute brain workout

3. Your 1-minute implementation exercise

4. Help! Why is my teenager acting this way? Background information and knowledge into why this may be happening and what you can do to ease the strain.

5. Help! It has all gone wrong! What to do if things don't quite go the way you planned.

6. Extra Credit – for those parents who are ultra brave and want to take it even further.

As always, it is up to you how you work through the chapter, there are no hard and fast rules and each person will work at their own pace and in their own manner. Take what resonates most for you from this lesson and start there.

The questions in each chapter are designed to allow you to self-coach and will deepen the learning and experience for you.

How to punish and be tough without destroying the relationship

OK, I have a little confession to make. I am not going to teach you how to punish, but I will teach you how to be tough, stick to your word and ensure you teach your child responsibility. I think we live in a world that is all about winning, getting one over on another person and being right. There appears to be little room for compromise, understanding and agreeing. Nowhere to me does this seem to be more relevant than in the relationships with our children. "Because I told you so!" is a phrase so often used and I so often hear parents use the words battle, win and enemy when I hear them refer to their teenagers. I have to say, it really worries me. We are not at war with our teenager (although it may feel like that); we are just living with someone who has a different perspective to us and may not always do as we say all the time. Is that really a bad thing? Inevitably, when we live in close proximity with other people, there are bound to be times when we all get a little fraught with each other.

However, in these moments is it right for us to say, "You know what, I am the adult and you will do as I say!" Do we really have the right to control another person? Would it not be more productive to think about how the family, as a team, can agree on something that makes everyone feel better? This kind of thinking will move your relationship forward, keeping the lines of communication open, teaching your teenager a valuable lesson that life is not really about controlling others, it is about negotiating and coming to a compromise. I think that when it comes to teens we use the word punishment and discipline far too liberally. We believe that punishment is the only way to teach our children to behave in a way we want. And before the teen years, while this system may have not been the most effective, it has largely produced results mainly due to the fact that children are younger, smaller and easier to manipulate. However, as soon as that abstract thought starts to develop and our teens start to grow, they really do begin to question this element of control over them. Think of it; when you were punished did it really make you learn anything or did it just make your angry and want to seek revenge? Well, guess what? Nothing has changed and far from doing what you want it to do, punishment only has one effect and that is to aggravate your teenager and make them hate you, if only for a short moment. Don't get me wrong here, I am not saying that your teen should get away with everything they do and run riot, what I am saying is that you need to be firm and fair and remember that your job is to teach them and that they learn from their mistakes. Grounding is not something that happens in the real world and I think we mostly wish that we just got sent to our rooms nowadays when something went wrong. We punish and control our teenager for many reasons, mainly because we think that is what works and that is the mindset that we all have and also because perhaps we were controlled and we think that is the way. Sometimes, because we lack respect and self esteem in ourselves, controlling others makes us feel good. When our child disagrees with us or says no, we can take that far too personally, think it is about us and respond from a personal place. Let me tell you, nobody will win that way. The way to be tough with your child without ruining the relationship is to be clear, firm and fair, all the time knowing what it is you want as a parent. No one says it better in my mind that William Glasser, who says you can only hold a gun at someone's head for so long before they no longer care if you shoot.

When dealing with any misdemeanours, we need to think before we react and that is the most important thing. So often in these kinds of situations we are driven by our feelings and it is like being stuck in the mud; our wheels are spinning but we are going nowhere. We need to get ourselves out of the feelings, as that will force us to make really silly and emotional, driven decisions which are bound to cause conflict in any home. People and situations are so much more complicated than quick fix, punishment style approaches. If we want to improve the situations in our home then we must realise that it may take as long to improve as it did to break down in the first place. People only change when they are ready to and most of the time, this is not quick!

Our children are not appliances, something cannot just break and you call in someone to repair it. It is like an exercise programme; it is painful, sometimes goes off track, can go for ages without any results and it takes time to achieve your outcome. I believe that positive relationships are the key to any long-lasting change. If we want to influence and impact our children to do right so we stop having to punish them when they do wrong, then we must ensure that we build our relationships with them over anything else. It is so easy for us to focus on measurement, behaviour and attitude. So easy for us to look outside and blame our child for a result that we find undesirable. It a takes a strong, courageous person to look inside and say, "What am I doing that is not allowing this person to shine?"

Our intentions for our children should not be based upon how to get this person to do what you want but by asking whether what you are about to do is going to harm or damage the relationship. To influence a young person we must be in what is known as a sphere of influence. As a teacher, a parent or employer, we need to be in this sphere if we are to effect any change and support this young person to be who we know they can be. We can only do this if we have a strong relationship with them. A strong relationship can achieve ten times more than any reward or punishment. Our relationship with our child should be based upon seeing a real human being and all the potential within, not just what they are doing at that precise moment. We should see the qualities in them and not just the behaviour in front of us. These relationships must be based on trust, understanding and equality. We have no right to control another person through rewards, punishment, blaming or shaming. These practices will not produce long term success.

We need to love rather than hate, be firm and compassionate over blaming and shaming and above all, set clear agreements and boundaries in participation with the young people themselves. We need to start doing with our children rather than to them.

However, saying all that from my soap box, I also know that we need to ensure our children learn responsibility and being part of a family, with all that involves. That is why I created my agreement system. Making agreements with your children is a way to instil responsibility, while also keeping the relationship intact.

Agreements alone can solve many problems in a less than harmonious household.

There are three steps in making agreements with your teenagers.

Step One

Before all else, you must be clear in your own mind about the result you want, about what you are trying to achieve.

Step Two

Make the request by outlining what you want to do and ask for an agreement to be discussed and reached. At the asking point you may get a yes. You can then get on with reaching some form of agreement. You may get a no or a maybe; at either of these you must stand firm, remember what result you want to achieve, don't accept less and don't negotiate beyond it.

Step Three

You and your teenager must both be clear about what is to be done, when it is to be done. A useful ploy is to write it down, make lists.

Agreements are great because they make young people part of any solution.

There are so many interventions at the moment that do to our young people rather than with them. They need to be engaged, consulted and included in any decisions that are made about them. Participation is the key to change. Only through participation will we get a very clear understanding of the challenges and problems and be able to support children to go about finding their own solutions.

Your 3-minute emotional workout

For me, working on your emotional stuff is the key to being a strong and powerful parent. However, it is not easy. When you are doing these emotional exercises, don't get too involved with what comes up. Just notice that it is interesting and let it go. We have a tendency to 'navel gaze', feel sorry and think there is something wrong with us. We all have stuff - emotional baggage - and to move forward all we have to do is notice it and move on.

Firstly, I want you to find a quiet space where you will not be disturbed and take three deep breaths; this will just balance you.

Then I just want you to sit with these three questions. Just ask them of yourself and notice what comes up in terms of thoughts, feelings and emotions.

1. When you think about not being able to control others, how does it make you feel?

2. How did your parents control you?

3. Do you feel in control of your own life?

If you get nothing coming up then that is fine too, just come back to it another day.

Just sit for three minutes and after that, have a notebook to hand and just quickly jot down the thoughts, feelings or emotions that comes up for you.

Your two minute thinking exercise.

Your two minute thinking exercise.

I say 'thinking', but I am going to be asking you to write too.

Getting all the feelings out to do with a situation will really support you in moving forward.

Get a pen and paper and the pad you used to jot down your observations from the above exercise.

Then just answer these questions on the paper; write as much or as little as you feel.

1. What was the one thought, feeling or emotion stuck in my mind from the previous exercise?

2. What makes this so poignant for me?

3. How is it impacting my relationship with my child now?

Then just sit, take a few breaths and release.

Your implementation exercise.

Make one agreement with your child.

Help! Why is my teenager acting this way?

No one likes being controlled, so when we try and do it to our teenager, is it any wonder that they rebel? As abstract thought develops, your teenager starts to realise that they have a voice and they want a say. They start to think that they are important and they start to question things they may not have questioned before. This abstract thought process has them thinking about things in a different way and feeling that they are able to speak out for what they think is fair. Abstract thought gives them a much broader perspective and sense of justice. So, where before they may have gone along with a situation, they will now make it clear that they don't agree, or don't think it is fair. This is all part of learning to become an adult.

Help! It has all gone wrong!

OK, the very first thing you need to do when things go wrong is to be driven by your feelings and don't panic.

Facts and Feelings

When you find yourself feeling frustrated, angry, upset and annoyed by what your teenager is doing, go to this part of the book and do this process.

What is the situation:

....

Think about the situation and ask yourself what the facts are, for example, your teenager shouted and swore at you. Then ask yourself what the feelings are; you may for instance feel that your teen doesn't care what you think. Think of all you can and write them under two headings.

Facts

Feelings

Now just look at the facts and for each one think of one thing you can go and do about it now. One solution you could put in place that would deal with that fact, for example, your child shouted at you, so you will tell them that this is not acceptable.

When you have found a solution for each one, decide which one you want to implement and go and do it.

Keep doing this process again and again and it will move you forward; if you let yourself get stuck in the feelings, then nothing will change.

When things go wrong, follow my belief that people do not fail, systems fail. I really believe that when we see failure in our young people it is down to a weakness in a system, be it a school system, a family system or a societal system. As people, we want to succeed and to succeed we need to find the right system and environment for us to do that. Families argue because their communication and organisational systems could do with some work. Where you see an agreement fail, I urge you to think 'system failure', not people failure. Remember, people do not want to fail; it is just that we have just not found the conditions/systems yet to help them succeed. After over seventeen years of working in this field I have yet to find a situation that could not be made better by tweaking an existing system or putting a new one in place. These systems may need to be tweaked, revamped and changed constantly and this is part of the process. Everyone cannot fit into the same system and be successful.

So, first look at your agreement you made; was it crystal clear or does it need tweaking at all to make it more effective?

A lot of the time we really do set our children up to fail. We give them a job to do or agree on what chores they will be responsible for and then chastise them when they don't deliver to our standards. So what is missing, where did it all go wrong? Well, quite simply, you didn't give them any guidelines. Imagine that you go into an office one day and in front of you are some papers and envelopes. You arrive and they tell you that your job is just to put the papers in the envelopes. You do as asked and after completing the job you proudly tell them you have finished, only to be told that the paper is in the wrong way and they needed four pages in each. How are you feeling? Pretty angry I guess, and you want to scream, "Why didn't you tell me that?" This is exactly my point. You cannot blame your child for a job badly done if you have not told them how; you have to get very, very specific. Just saying that they need to clean up the bathroom may not be enough. You may need to make them a checklist of what cleaning the bathroom entails, guidelines to help them complete the job. Just think of the word guidance and what it means – leadership, instruction and direction and all too often, this is where parents slip up. If you are teaching your child about money and they have a certain amount each week, then you need to give them guidelines about what that money is for, how long it is meant to last and what happens when it runs out. If you child wants their friend to come over that is great, but you need guidelines. Don't expect you teenager to read your mind (yes, these aliens have incredible power, but it does not stretch that far!) or figure it out for themselves. You need to tell them. Most arguments in the house can be prevented with a little bit of guidance on your behalf.

If these were crystal clear and you think that they failed to fulfil their part of the bargain due to a blatant disrespect, then you will need to issue a consequence.

Consequences

Every action has a reaction and everything your teenager does will have a consequence, good or bad. What you need to make sure of is that when an agreement is broken that the consequence that follows is one from which your teenager can learn and grow. Not just a spur of the moment, 'I am going to take your TV away!' kind of thing. What most parents will resort to is a punishment. The teenager does not conform; they tell the teenager what is wrong and tell them that if they do not stop, they will be punished. The parent will make the judgment and enforce the punishment. Punishment takes responsibility away from the teenager and does not allow them to choose a better course of action. William Glasser describes punishment as, "A gun being pointed at a teenager's head to motivate him." He goes on to say that this is ineffective as the teenager will only conform while the gun is pointed at them. When it is lowered, the motivation to do the right thing goes away or even worse, they get so used to the fear of the gun that it is no longer effective. All punishment does is teach a teenager to conform rather than thinking and taking responsibility for themselves. I suggest that you take your time to think of the consequences and give yourself at least 24 hours before discussing anything with your teenager. Some agreements will have natural consequences, like lateness for school, and some may not. Always think about what you are trying to teach your teenager and respond from that place. If you are trying to teach them responsibility, then the consequence needs to relate to that. When it comes to consequences, then I want you to think in terms of penalties and remedies.

Penalties

I thought long and hard before using this word. In its broadest term it does mean punishment, which is something that I don't agree with, since it does not promote learning. However, on further investigation I found that it also means loss or another unfortunate result of one's actions, which I do think fits with what we are talking about here. If you child breaks an agreement or does something that is less than desirable, then chances are there will be some kind of loss or unfortunate result. If we don't turn up for work, then we may get fired. If your child is late for school, they may get a detention. There is always some consequence that will be natural and this may be enough, however sometimes you as a parent may also need to step in and issue a penalty. So this is how I want you to look at it, something happens and an agreement is broken and there is natural consequence for that. It is then your job as a parent to decide whether you to also need to issue a penalty. If your child was caught by the police a stint in the cells may be enough. However, if they are late for school a detention may not do the job. You then need to ask yourself, "What is the remedy here?" This is the first important step. So if your child is late for school, the remedy may be that he can no longer set his bedtime and you set it for a few weeks. In order to do that you may have to issue a penalty of taking the TV and Play Station out of the room. You would only issue the penalty, however, if the remedy has not worked. So think of this as a three-step process. I suggest that the first time this happens you let the natural consequence be enough and only if it happens again do you move on. You then ask yourself what the remedy to this problem is, you implant that and if that does not work, then step in with a penalty. The very best thing to do is discuss these with your teenager, so that they get a say and they know the score; sometimes, though, you will just have to step in.

Remedies

A remedy is something that you put in place to "cure", a constant challenge with your teenager. What I ask you to do here is this: when your teenager does something wrong, instead of punishing them, first ask yourself, and then them, what the remedy is. At the end of the day I am assuming that you want the situation to improve. To do that you need to put a remedy in place first. So before you think anything, think remedy.

Extra Credit

Do you really want to take this further? Start introducing clear boundaries in your home.

You make agreements about the boundaries in the house. I prefer to use the words boundary instead of rule; to me a rule is a very rigid word and promotes ideas of authority and regulations and will send any teenager, or adult for that matter, into rebellion. It is natural behaviour for us to want to break the rules that someone else has imposed on us, we only have to look at the title of Marcus Buckingham and Curt Coffman's book, First Break all the Rules, to know this is true of everyone. No one likes rules! A boundary to me is much more flexible and is an indication of the furthest limit that a person is prepared to go. It gives a teenager a limit to their behaviour rather than a rule to stick to.

Boundaries can be negotiated and agreed; rules are just set and adhered to. If you want cooperation from your teenagers then work with boundaries, not rules. Here is a little tip for you when agreeing boundaries – always offer up a boundary that is not your final limit; teenagers like to negotiate and will always push the boundaries a little. For example, if you want to set 10.30 as a time to come in, start negotiating at 9.30, be prepared to agree at about 10.00 and then be prepared to stretch it to 10.30. What this means is that your teenager will think they have won by making you agree to 10.00. They will then push it a little and be 10 minutes late, just because they will do, but really you have won because you wanted 10.30. So you both have got what you want and it will be your little secret! You need to be prepared to be a little flexible and remember that, although it may feel like your teenager has had one over on you that actually, they haven't. If however, they do stretch the time and come in past 10.30, then you would need to step in, stating that it was unacceptable and issue a remedy or penalty. It is a very clever way of stopping conflicts while also getting what you want.

I suggest that parents set boundaries around these five areas.

Eating

Sleeping

Responsibilities – these are to include jobs and chores

Money

Behaviour

Be prepared to discuss these with your teenagers and negotiate agreements around each one.

Set at least one boundary around each of these areas and use agreements to get them clear, focused and agreed upon.

Week Eight

How to motivate and kick into action even the most disengaged teen.

Welcome to your eighth week in your programme. This week we will be working together to show you how to motivate and kick into action even the most disengaged teen.

This chapter contains:

1. Your 3-minute daily emotional workout

2. Your 2-minute brain workout

3. Your 1-minute implementation exercise

4. Help! Why is my teenager acting this way? Background information and knowledge into why this may be happening and what you can do to ease the strain.

5. Help! It has all gone wrong! What to do if things don't quite go the way you planned.

6. Extra Credit – for those parents who are ultra brave and want to take it even further.

As always, it is up to you how you work through the chapter; there are no hard and fast rule, each person will work at their own pace and in their own manner. Take what resonates most for you from this lesson and start there.

The questions in each chapter are designed to allow you to self-coach and will deepen the learning and experience for you.

How to motivate and kick into action even the most disengaged teen.

Let's face it, teenagers can lie in bed all day, seem not interested in anything and be extremely lazy. It can sometimes feel like you need a rocket to get them moving. Parents can become very frustrated when they find that all the hard work they have put into their teenager is wasted when he refuses to get out of bed, come away from the gaming machine or, heaven forbid, think about his future. It can feel as if teenagers spend all day on the sofa, expecting to be waited upon hand and foot.

All is not lost! I have worked with many teenagers and their parents in similar situations. They can be turned round. But first we need to give them a reason to change. I mean, if you could, wouldn't you want to lie in bed, do nothing and watch the TV? If you as the parent are always there, always letting them get away with it and saving them from failure, then why would they need motivation? Motivation in its simplest term is a motive to take action. If there is no motive, there will be no action. Simple!

A word on motivation.

When I am working with teenagers one of the first things I need to establish is how are they motivated. Are they motivated by pleasure or are they motivated by pain?

Pleasure, the joy of getting something and Pain, the hurt of not or the fear of ending up a certain way.

When I was young I was certainly motivated by pain. The pain that motivated me was that I didn't want to work in a factory in Scunthorpe, sewing knickers. All I knew was what I didn't want. I didn't want that, and it made me work harder.

You may have a child that wants a successful life with the Ferrari, the big house and all the rest of it. They are motivated by pleasure. Or you may have a child who does not want to do worse than their brother or end up going to the local college instead of the college of their choice.

Most people say they are motivated by pleasure, when actually it could be pain.

A motive to take action.

So if motivation is a motive to take action, then why isn't your teenager taking any?

Here are some common reasons I find.

1. They just are not interested or can't see the point.

This is a really challenging one and quite often stems around school work. Making someone interested in something they are not is nearly impossible; however, making someone see something as relevant is possible.

We need to ensure that our children realise they have a choice and that each choice means they are saying yes to something and no to something else. I find that this system works really well.

Let me give you an example.

My daughter came home and didn't want to do her Maths homework.

"Have you got any homework?"

"I think I have Maths, but I really can't be bothered"

"What is it you want to do instead?"

"Just go on the computer and stuff."

"So if you choose to say yes to the computer and no to Maths what might the consequences be?"

Bronte storms off to do her Maths homework.

You see, even my child storms off! The point here is that she made a choice to do her Maths homework without me having to nag. I just pointed out that it was a choice and if she made it, there would be consequences. The key here is to plant a seed and let it grow; it is the same with relevance. If they can't see how something is relevant, then asking a question such as, "I wonder how history is relevant to your life now?" or "What skills do you learn doing history?" are all good questions to get them thinking. One of the best ways to stop you nagging at them when they need to do something they are not interested in is to say, "That is your choice, however you must face the consequences of the choices you make."

2. They have no reason to take action things are easy and comfortable the way they are.

Here you need to be really truthful with yourself. Are you doing too much that is allowing your child to not need to be motivated? If your child knows that if they leave their college application you will eventually take charge of it, then why should they do anything? You have to be very brave here and willing to face the consequences of failure. Failure is, after all, the best way to have anyone learn what not to do.

You just need to be really clear what you will and will not do and give them the responsibility. For example, "The choice of college is yours and I trust you to make the right decision. I am handing over responsibility for this to you. I will not do anything else for this unless you ask me."

3. They know that you, their parents, will step in and save the day if it comes to crunch time.

I think the above example illustrates this really well. Most parents will, at the last minute, step in. From an early age my children have known that I won't - what I say is what I mean. Making empty threats about what you will do and then not doing it will never get your child into action. Letting your teenager know that when they leave school there will be a 50% cut in pocket money as they are expected to get a part time job will certainly spring them into action, especially if they know you will follow through.

4. They have no confidence due to not having to try on previous occasions.

I often hear parents and teens make the excuse of having no confidence to explain why they won't do something. I just don't buy it; to be honest I think what it really means is that they feel uncomfortable and don't like the feeling, having not had to push through it before and not wanting to now. When we get frightened and scared for our children and try and keep them so they don't fail or get hurt, we run the risk of making them feel they are not confident. When your child says that they can't, tell them they can. Ask them what they need to make this happen and if they ask you to do it for them, don't. Ask how you can support them instead.

My daughter recently wanted to supplement her pocket money and asked if we would call the local newsagents to see if there were any paper rounds, to which we replied,

"No, if you want the job, you make the phone call."

This was met with lots of pleas for us to do it for her, and the use of that face that only daughters know how to pull, to which we replied,

"We are willing to go with you to the newsagents but you will need to ask them."

To this day, she hasn't gone to ask and that is fine, the choice is hers. Yes, if we had stepped in she may have got a job, but why should I do something that she is more than capable of doing?

Your 3-minute emotional workout

For me, working on your emotional stuff is the key to being a strong and powerful parent. However, it is not easy. When you are doing these emotional exercises, don't get too involved with what comes up. Just notice that it is interesting and let it go. We have a tendency to 'navel gaze', feel sorry and think there is something wrong with us. We all have stuff - emotional baggage - and to move forward all we have to do is notice it and move on.

Firstly, I want you to find a quiet space where you will not be disturbed and take three deep breaths; this will just balance you.

Then I just want you to sit with these three questions. Just ask them of yourself and notice what comes up in terms of thoughts, feelings and emotions.

1.   How did your parents motivate you?

2. Were your bribed as a child and how did that make you feel?

3. Where are you doing too much for your children, so they don't have to be motivated?

If you get nothing coming up then that is fine too, just come back to it another day.

Just sit for three minutes and after that, have a notebook to hand and just quickly jot down the thoughts, feelings or emotions that comes up for you.

Your two minute thinking exercise.

Your two minute thinking exercise.

I say 'thinking', but I am going to be asking you to write too.

Getting all the feelings out to do with a situation will really support you in moving forward.

Get a pen and paper and the pad you used to jot down your observations from the above exercise.

Then just answer these questions on the paper; write as much or as little as you feel.

1. What was the one thought, feeling or emotion stuck in my mind from the previous exercise?

2. What makes this so poignant for me?

3. How is it impacting my relationship with my child now?

Then just sit, take a few breaths and release.

Your implementation exercise.

Is your child motivated by pleasure or pain? Listen to how they speak, what they say and how they get themselves into action

Help! Why is my teenager acting this way?

Motivation is a really tricky thing and something we need to learn. I don't believe we are born more motivated or less motivated than others, I just think our life experiences teach us how to motivate ourselves. Motivation with teens is even trickier, they find it hard to sleep, their brains are changing so much, their internal policeman has taken a break and they are learning that the real world is a little tougher than they previously thought. Being a motivated and joyous 10 or 11 year old is easy; no real pressure! When they hit the teens, though, it is much more difficult. Most parents take this sudden and swift change to mean that there is something wrong with their child, but often this is merely them dealing with their new thought processes, complex of relationships and the added school pressure. However, depression in teenagers is common, so if the symptoms persist and they are shutting themselves in their rooms for extended periods of time, then I suggest you seek medical help.

Is your child motivated by pleasure or pain? Listen to how they speak, what they say and how they get themselves into action

Help! It has all gone wrong!

How can it go wrong when motivation is a lifelong process?

If you have handed responsibility over to your teen and they didn't do anything, then go back and read the module on responsibility. You remember the laundry incident? Well, it is the same as that.

However, if you teenager is really disengaged then here are some tips for you.

1. Find some common ground – it is no good approaching this child from your own point of view, you need to approach them from a place that they can communicate from, something that they understand, be it music, popular culture, TV, whatever it is, find some common ground.

2. Love them more than they hate themselves. It is about seeing beyond what is in front of you and seeing what lies beneath; seeing possibilities, not problems.

3. See their faults and ask what they need –what is it really that this young person in front of you needs?

4. Be honest open and relax; young people can see straight through you.

Extra Credit

I want you to look at how you are motivated because how we are motivated will often be how we motivate others.

Take a look at the Enneagram. It is a tool I love. You can take a free test on-line and see what you come out as. Read the other descriptions; what types do you think your children are? How might you be trying to motivate them from your perspective and not theirs?

Think about the following questions

1. How do you motivate yourself?

2. Do you give yourself permission to have a day off when you don't feel up to it? Do you allow your teen the same?

3. How are you trying to motivate your teen at the moment?

4. How do you think you could try and motivate them more effectively?

Week Nine

Sure-fire ways to get what you need done without resorting to shouting.

This Chapter is going to be slightly different in that it won't follow the previous one. In this chapter, I am going to go through my favourite and most often used techniques. These are the techniques I use in my own home and in the homes of my clients. Some we may have been through before, some will be new, but what they all have in common is that they will help you get done in your home what needs to be done without resorting to shouting. I think it is great to recap and go over what we can do and if you get nothing else from this book, I want you to take away these tools.

Agreements

I am starting with what I think is one of the most important things to create a stress free family; agreements. Agreements alone can solve many problems in a less than harmonious household. I think we live in a world that is all about winning, getting one over on another person and being right. There appears to be little room for compromise, understanding and agreeing. Nowhere to me does this seem to be more relevant than in the relationships with our children. "Because I told you so!" is a phrase so often used and I so often hear parents use the words battle, win and enemy when I hear them refer to their teenagers. I have to say, it really worries me. We are not at war with our teenager; (although it may feel like that) we are just living with someone who has a different perspective to us and may not always do as we say all the time. Is that really a bad thing?

Inevitably, when we live in close proximity with other people, there are bound to be times when we all get a little fraught with each other. However, in these moments is it right for us to say, "You know what, I am the adult and you will do as I say!" Do we really have the right to control another person? Would it not be more productive to think about how the family, as a team, can agree on something that makes everyone feel better? This kind of thinking will move your relationship forward, keeping the lines of communication open, teaching your teenager a valuable lesson that life is not really about controlling others, it is about negotiating and coming to a compromise.

There are three steps in making agreements with your teenagers.

Step One

Before all else, you must be clear in your own mind about the result you want, about what you are trying to achieve.

Step Two

Make the request by outlining what you want to do and ask for an agreement to be discussed and reached. At the asking point you may get a yes. You can then get on with reaching some form of agreement. You may get a no or a maybe; at either of these you must stand firm, remember what result you want to achieve, don't accept less and don't negotiate beyond it.

Step Three

You and your teenager must both be clear about what is to be done, when it is to be done. A useful ploy is to write it down, make lists.

Boundaries

Boundaries go hand and hand with agreements. You make agreements about the boundaries in the house. I prefer to use the words boundary instead of rule; to me a rule is a very rigid word and promotes ideas of authority and regulations and will send any teenager, or adult for that matter, into rebellion. It is natural behaviour for us to want to break the rules that someone else has imposed on us, we only have to look at the title of Marcus Buckingham and Curt Coffman's book, First Break all the Rules, to know this is true of everyone. No one likes rules!

A boundary to me is much more flexible and is an indication of the furthest limit that a person is prepared to go. It gives a teenager a limit to their behaviour rather than a rule to stick to. Boundaries can be negotiated and agreed, rules are just set and adhered to. If you want cooperation from your teenagers then work with boundaries, not rules.

Choice

I am such a fan of choice, what it promotes and the results it generates. As adults we are faced with choices every day yet quite often, we do not allow our children the same privilege, telling them where and when they must do something, in our efforts to control them. Recently I was working with a twelve-year-old who was refusing to go to school and had not been for seven months. Her family, very concerned, just kept telling her had to go and the more they told her, the more she stuck her heels in. I asked her what her choices were in this situation; she stated that staying at home was her only choice. I then asked her what other choices there were and together we came up with a list of four other choices - on-line school, home tutors, going back to her old school or picking a new school. She initially opted for the on-line school and within a week we had her learning again. Every time she asked me what I thought she should do, I just told her that the choice was hers and that I trusted her to do what was right. After a month she said she was ready to go back to her old school and I can state that as of today, she has successfully spent a week at school. The point is, it was her choice that she came to by herself; by taking the pressure of her and the rest of the family and putting the choice back onto her. She did what was right. When you are struggling with one of your teenager's issues, go through the choices with them, tell them the choice is theirs and you trust them to do what is right. Then watch them squirm. They find this concept so difficult, since they are so used to being told what to do and having something to fight against, that they are not sure what to do and most will eventually make a good choice. You just need to get off their back and allow them the time.

There are a few other ways you can use this tool. Instead of saying, "Tom, go and do the washing up now!" you can say, "Tom, you can do the washing up now or after this TV programme, which do you choose?" You are giving him choice but also making sure that what needs to be done, gets done.

"Tom, your dinner will be on the table in five minutes. You can come down now or later, however I will not heat it up or cook you anything else later, the choice is yours."

Whenever you are in any conflict with your teenager, think how you can give them a choice that will also get done what needs to be done. Just think what a valuable life lesson you are teaching them.

Questions

Questions can be a very powerful way to turn around any situation and take the heat out. If your teen is getting frustrated about something and taking it out on you, ask a question like, "What would you like me to do, or how can I solve this?" This is a very empowering way to not get involved in a row and shift your teenager to finding a solution. They may not answer the question or you may be met with a grunt of, "I don't know". That is fine; just asking someone a question moves them from the problem to beginning to find a solution.

Questions to think about.

Have you tried all these tools?

What worked best and what didn't work?

What will you do next time?

How can you improve and what you have already done?

How has your relationship with your teenager improved?

Week Ten

How to enjoy being with your teenager and have some fun!

Think about it; what do teenagers bring to the world, if not fun?

They know how to have a good time and live in the moment. As adults, there is a lot we can learn from that. Put a bit of fun back into your relationship and communicate with your teenager at the level they are at. So often, every time parents talk to their teenagers it is either to tell them off, to talk about their future or some other thing the child is not doing the way the parents would wish. They never appear to have small talk, laugh or chat about anything fun.

It appears that in the teen years we get very serious and think we need to be very serious about bringing up our children. Yes things get a bit tenser, yes things get a bit more grown up, but do they have to get serious?

I think fun is a vital part of any relationship. When we can laugh and have fun together, we can get through most things. However, teenagers are slippery characters and one thing that may have made them laugh one day makes them cross the next. Things that they loved before the teen's years are suddenly very boring. Things you used to enjoy together, they are no longer willing to participate in.

Lots of things change in the teen years that contribute to this. Dopamine levels (the fun chemical) in their brain decreases, meaning that to get the same kick they have to do things that are more and more risky, which is why things they liked earlier no longer interest them. Their peers become much more important to them and trying to work out their identity and where they belong in the world becomes much more important than spending time with their parents.

Most parents can take this very personally and see it as their teen not liking them anymore, but that simply isn't true, so don't give up. Even if your teen has said no to something hundreds of time before, keep asking, because you never know one day, they may say yes. When you ask and they say no, don't say something like, "Please yourself, you never do anything with us anymore," but respond by saying something like, "That is a real shame because I love spending time with you". Don't ever give up.

There are a few things you can do in your home to instil a bit of fun.

1. On days off, round the breakfast table, ask everyone what fun thing they would like to do today; tell them what you want to do. Then look at the day and see what you can fit in. Just even mentioning and suggesting that there could be something fun to do could warm your teenager to the

idea. If you don't get an answer, don't make them wrong for that, just carry on.

2. In holidays, make your teen the fun or entertainment manager. Give them the responsibility for ensuring you do all the things that everyone wants to. Set them a budget and have them come up with an entertainment plan that everyone will want to participate in.

3. Start a fun bowl. In our house we have a glass bowl called the fun bowl. In the fun bowl are pieces of paper that have things written on. We have each written on ten pieces of paper fun things we want to do and when anyone says they are bored, we pull one out and we all have to do it. There are things from having a party to preparing an Oscar speech and a ton of things in between. We each pick one out then, as a family, agree which we want to do. 80% of them cost no money. It is a great way to bring spontaneity into a family and ensure you get to spend time together.

I think what parents have most trouble with is the inconsistency in teenagers. One day they can laugh at your jokes and the next it is 'lame' and as parents, we never know which mood our teenager is in and we end up putting our foot in it. To counteract this in my home, I started a weather board. It was simple; a plain broad with everyone's name on, alongside four symbols:

Sunny - this stood for - I am in a real happy mood

Stormy - I am feeling quite angry - just keep your distance

Cloudy - I am OK, not in the best of moods but not angry either

Rainy - I am feeling emotional today and a little sad.

Each day we simply put the symbol that represented our mood near our name and changed it throughout the day as we wanted. This meant that we all knew how to approach each other. We would sometimes also tell others what weather we were for the day over breakfast. This was of course for the teenagers' benefit more than anyone else's. Teenagers' mood are notorious volatile and quick to change and this allowed us all to approach in the manner appropriate to the mood. I have since implemented this in many family's homes and it worked just as well as it did in ours. It just helps everyone to understand each other and to ensure that you don't unnecessarily cause more conflict.

Use the moments you have with them to have conversations that don't make them wrong, are light and above all, bring an element of fun to them. Doing fun things together, I think, is imperative for any family and don't just judge the things that you think of as fun; as we have learnt in some case studies, what you think is fun may be your teenagers idea of hell! Ask them what they would like to do and accommodate that. Give your teenager the job of social secretary in the house and let them organise the things you all do together, with some guidelines of course.

Humour is a great healer and fun and laughter can get us though even the most difficult and trying times. Don't underestimate simply laughing and enjoying each other's company.

Thank You

Thank you so much for taking the time to read this book. I do hope you have implemented the tips in it and have found improvement in your home.

I always love to hear from my readers, so please feel free to send me an e-mail at sarah@sarahnewton.com.

Wishing you all the best.

Have fun

Sarah

More about Sarah

Teenologist, Celebrity Parent Coach, Speaker and Family Peacemaker

Hailed as "The Supernanny for Teens " by TV Times

Sarah Newton has been helping youth and families for over 17 years of her life, initially as a police officer in the Met and for the last 10 years running her own youth consultancy business.

She has worked with and transformed some of the most difficult and empathetic young people and regularly appears in the media, giving her expert opinion. She has been featured on most UK TV channels (with one of her programmes watched by 1 in 4 of the UK population), hosted her own TV series (which has aired in America, Australia, New Zealand, Poland and Scandinavia), been involved with campaigns for such companies as MTV, Paramount and the BBC and has sat on future thought panels for ITV.

Her first book, "Help! My Teenager is an Alien – the everyday situation guide for parents" was launched in March 2007. This book has now been translated into Polish and Chinese.

Whilst Sarah has a natural flair and pragmatic approach to resolving issues, she has been diligent in developing her professional skills. She has been professionally trained through Coach U, Comprehensive Coaching U and was the first U.K. graduate of the Academy of Family Coach Training. Sarah is currently getting certificated in the teaching of William Glasser's Choice Theory.

She combines this knowledge with her police experience all mixed together with equal parts of sensitivity, wonder, common sense, and humour to touch people's lives.

Sarah is passionate about educating, enabling and empowering young people to make better choices. Choices that are better for them, their families, their friends and society as a whole. She is a strong proponent of taking personal responsibility for our lives and the decisions we make. She is driven by a desire to help adults create environments and conditions that allow youth to thrive. This desire drove her to join forces with Lisa Warner, 2009 Entrepreneur of the Year, to educate families on communication skills.

Sarah is considered a thought leader among her peers and her futuristic attitude allows clients to benefit from her forward thinking, whole-person approach to everything she does. Her love of restorative justice and her obsession for information on generational theory, neuroscience and technology are slowly turning her into a closet Geek! Sarah is also the creator of the exciting new Teenology Model and the editor and creator of Celebrity Parent Advice.

Sarah lives happily in Northampton, England with her two daughters Bronte (15) and Freya (11), her husband and a menagerie of animals.

www.sarahnewton.com